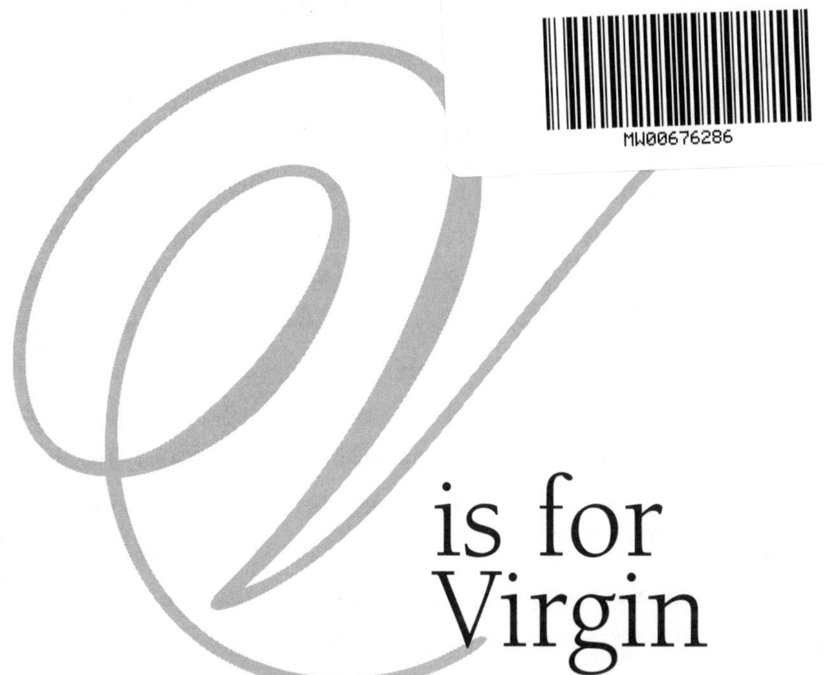

is for Virgin

The Unplugged Guide to Abstinence & Celibacy

by CHIQUITA LOCKLEY

Jamarl Publishing

All scripture quotations are taken from
the *King James Version* of the Bible.

Lyrics from India.Arie's "Video" used by permission,
Cazzydog Management.

V is for Virgin
The Unplugged Guide to Abstinence and Celibacy
ISBN 0-9719818-7-6

Published by Jamarl Publishing
Decatur, Georgia 30035
Printed in the United States of America.

Printed in the United States of America.

This book is dedicated to my grandparents —
James and Margaret Lockley,
whose sacrifices to give me a wonderful life
are as numerous as the stars in the sky.

and

To the memory of my niece, Kai L'Ani Ross,
who introduced me to a different kind of love.

~ But lay up for yourselves treasures in heaven…
for where your treasure is,
there will your heart be also ~

(Matthew 6:20-21)

is for Virgin

The Unplugged Guide to Abstinence & Celibacy

www.VisforVirgin.com

Contents

Acknowledgements

When God gave me the vision for this book, I was in a place where I could hear Him and receive His word. The reason that I was in such a place of quiet is because of the angels He placed around me to keep me on track.

To my mother, Charlene, for the sacrifices you made. To Aunt Linda, who taught me the basic principles of finance and all the rules for taking care of myself. To Grandma and Daddy, for instilling morals in me, and teaching me by example what it's like to share my life (house, food, and just everything) with others — for giving me first-hand experience in the spirit of hospitality. To Jesse, Bertha, Brenda, Fritz, Kelly, and Liz for treating me like a princess from day one. To Don, for taking time to make me learn from your mistakes — I know you thought I wasn't listening, but I was! To Latesha, my sister and co-publisher, thanks for dealing with my *emotions*. To my cousins — all of you — Tammy, Margaret, Roshare', Geno, Shania, Natasha, Tequira, Brent, Jess, Cierra, Mario, Anthony, Markekeen, Marvionna, Quez, Tanji, Kiki, Lon, and Remanda — for sharing my world and keeping me grounded. And to my nephew, David Benjamin — you are my sunshine!

To Santina Reynolds Ingram and Felicia Holmes Sharpe, who have taken the time to listen to my *issues* for over 2 decades now. To Daphne Jones, Rachael Johnson, Jasmine Morton Ross, Erica Brown, Tamara Stewart, Gena Taylor — my shrinks. To Alex Hickman, Andre Hickman, Jesse Owens, Aisha Anderson (my unofficial editor), Ayo Williams, Nichole Tilman, Ivy Simmons, Ceylon Copes, Nicole Martin, Malene Jackson, Joy Andrews, Tracy Adams, Piper Miller, Caryn Johnson, Amika King, Phylicia Fant, Keshia Knight-Pulliam, Whitney Benta, Gina Loring, and my line sisters, APEX 34, who always had the right words of encouragement for me ("Quita, you're not finished with that book YET?"). To Taft Q. Heatley, Leah Gray, Sheronn Williams, and Fe Baptiste for your unyielding support. To Lili, Jamar, Rasheed, PJ, Kristel, and the PK Connection — thnx! To Andrew Momon and Eric Burton for your **invaluable** assistance.

To Tina McElroy Ansa — for watering the seed and watching the flower grow.

To the doctors in my life, who reached into the recesses of their minds to help with the more technical aspect of this book, Rana Snipe Berry and Maia McCuiston Jackson. To Jasmine Coleman, for your research assistance.

To Bishop Eddie L. Long & Elder Vanessa Long, William & Danielle Murphy, eDDie Velez, Robin May, Lisa Bolden, Terrell Murphy, Tommy Powell, Kevin Bond, and the New Birth Family for the spiritual guidance and fellowship that is so vital in my life. To ROC Nation Youth Choir, my BABIES!!! To Mrs. Kay Jakes, Charlene Brown, and Miss Sharon for ALWAYS speaking words of life into me.

To Jeanine Cooper Taylor, an angel sent straight from God to encourage me with just the right words always at just the right time. Thank you so much.

And finally, to Sheri Huguely who spoke the words that made my baby jump. You awoke in me a dormant gift from God, and I am forever grateful for your obedience in admonishing me to give the desires of my heart back to Him — a concept that kept me up until sunrise. Thank you.

And to my Lord and Savior, Jesus Christ — without whom I am absolutely nothing, in whose presence I long to abide. Thank you for the gift of words.

— CL

Foreword

"Virginity is much like integrity — you can only lose it once and from that moment on, everything else changes." One of my spiritual sons shared this quote with me one day and it spoke volumes to me as I started assessing life, love and leadership. You know, we as preachers and ministers often teach abstinence and celibacy from the pulpit, but rarely give our young adults and teenagers a practical outline for keeping their virginity and saving themselves for marriage.

Now more than ever, society has begun to look at sex and sexual relationships without calculating the spiritual implications and consequences. *V is for Virgin* is an extraordinary book by an exceptional author that celebrates celibacy through nine dynamic chapters. In a day when our youth are bombarded with sexually explicit images and a degrading idea of women, it has become imperative that we as leaders, teachers, but most importantly as Christians, instill a sense of value and self-worth in our young women and men.

In her first book, author Chiquita Lockley has masterfully depicted sex, virginity, and celibacy from a spiritual perspective while writing to an audience of women who so desperately need to read these realistic words of life and encouragement. This book is sure to captivate and motivate women of all ages, ethnicities and cultures.

V is for Virgin transcends all barriers and stereotypes derived by modern media through an intense look at the scriptures, real-life situations and real-life consequences as it relates to premarital sex and sexual relationships. From STDs to hormones, *V is for Virgin* tackles it all and puts into words what we as adults often find impossible to articulate. Chiquita sets up seven practical rules and guidelines for readers to follow as they continue to live a fasted life and abstain from sex until God brings them the mate He has chosen.

May God bless you and your household as you are ministered to by this outstanding literary work. Chiquita has been blessed to share a word with the women of the world through this dynamic book. God has raised her up for such a time as this! I am blessed to know her as a daughter and fellow servant of the Lord.

— BISHOP EDDIE L. LONG

Introduction

Have you ever been in a place where it just seemed impossible to stand? Impossible to continue to walk in a Godly way and be the daughter He's ordained for you to be? Well this is where I found myself in my walk of abstinence, so I thought that if I could just find a book that would speak to my needs and give me some advice on how to continue my walk, then I'd be able to make it just a little longer... Well, much to my chagrin, when I went to find this book that could talk to me — a twenty six year old virgin very much in tune with reality, there was almost nothing!!!

Please tell me how I'm supposed to continue saying no to all these beautiful men in Atlanta when there's no guide! No manual? No road map? How am I supposed to withstand the *cut up* when everywhere I turn, I see them? They're on every T.V. channel, cable or not. Try to find a station that doesn't feature the abs of Tyson Beckford or the smile of Usher Raymond. They sing the songs that we love and are featured in the magazines that we read. So, where is help when you need it? Who's around to say "I did it and so can you"? Nobody…that was my answer. Now, I'm sitting here and it comes to me that maybe I, the self-proclaimed goddess of Virginity, should bestow upon myself the role of *drawer of the map*, the Virgin's guide to Abstaining.

The next few pages are just the rules that have gotten me to the place of abstinence where I am. It's these notions that I submit to you as my personal road map in times of distress and duress. Some of these instructions will make you laugh, while others will make you cry, but through it all, you will be a little closer to the goal of keeping your virginity in tact. As you forage for guidelines along the bumps and curves of this sometimes-tumultuous road to success, keep your road map out. You're gonna need it!!! Have a safe trip and Enjoy!

CHIQUITA LOCKLEY — *Goddess of Virginity*

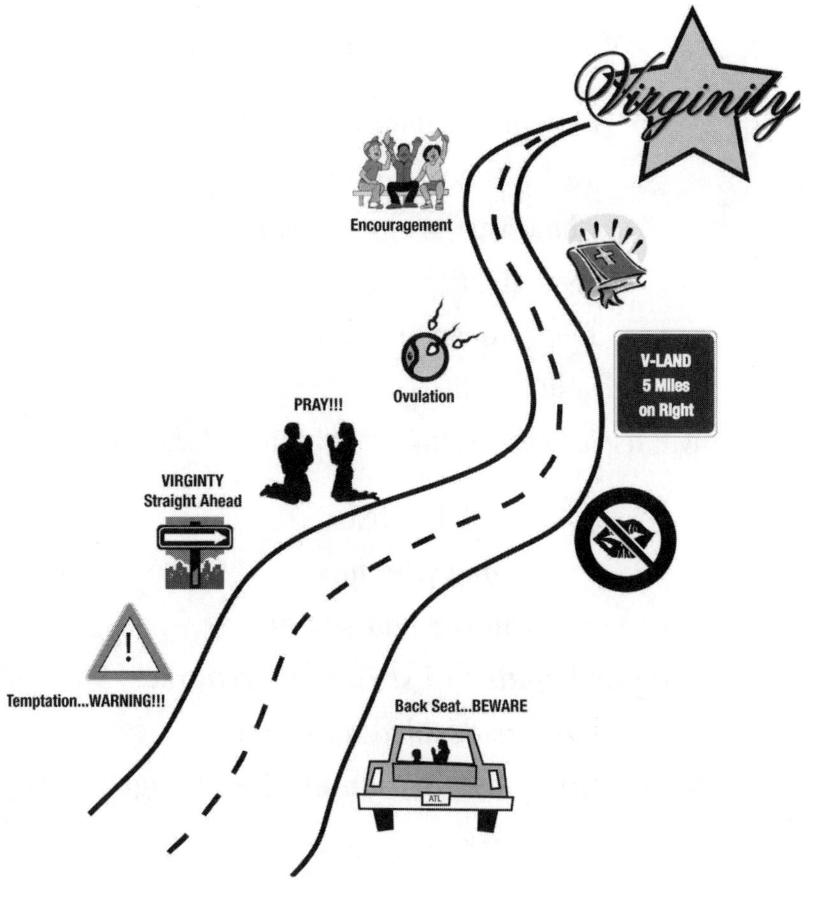
Virginity
Encouragement
Ovulation
PRAY!!!
V-LAND
5 Miles
on Right
VIRGINTY
Straight Ahead
Temptation...WARNING!!!
Back Seat...BEWARE
ATL

Virgin Disclaimer:

A virgin is defined as a person
who has not had sex before;
however, for the purposes
of disseminating vital information
to all women who are trying
to walk in a lifestyle of abstinence,
we will use a more inclusive definition of the term.

VIRGIN:
one who has
a) never had sex or
b) participated in sexual intercourse,
but has decided to abstain
from future participation until marriage.

Over the course of my life, I have met many women who have reclaimed their virginity (although some of them prefer not to use the title, but rather one of "celibacy"). There are many reasons why women have sex, and there are many reasons why some of them choose to stop having sex. Whatever your personal situation may be on this journey of abstinence, I hope the following words offer help and hope. Congratulations on your U-turn!

And to those of you who have become sexually active by force, not choice, I pray that these words offer comfort and make your walk of abstinence a little bit easier. When others have power and control issues and use our bodies as pawns in their sick games, the victims are left with all sorts of emotions, ranging from rage to emptiness to self-deprecation to powerlessness and vulnerability. You're also left with a taste — the flavor of sex. Although sex may not have been your "choice", you have definitely tasted the fruit and may face more challenges than the next person. If this is your situation, I pray that you've sought counseling/restoration and are using this book as a tool to maintain your walk of abstinence. If you haven't dealt with the deeper issues of your situation, I urge you to contact your local RAPE counselors, or RAINN (**R**ape **A**buse **I**ncest **N**ational **N**etwork) at 1 800 656-HOPE.

CHAPTER 1

The Games We Play & More

In life there are so many ambiguities and gray areas that it makes it very difficult for one to know the truth when she is faced with it. The courts tell us that marijuana is an illegal drug substance, but it's one of the easiest drugs for teens to possess. The churches admonish against homosexuality, yet the choir stands and pews are home to many gays and lesbians. And to add more confusion to this already confusing world, we are left here to make heads and tails out of our hormones. We're taught growing up that sex is an act that's for adults in mature situations, but in every video, teen sex is apparent. So what's a young woman to do when she finds herself in the gray area? Some would say pray, and this is definitely an option, but don't think for one moment that prayer alone will help you make the decision to abstain. It is only part of the equation to supporting your decision of actively pursuing abstinence.

So let's just get to the point. In this quest for abstinence, there comes into play the gray area, also known as The GAME. This GAME can appear in several different forms, including the tease, petting, oral sex, the test drive, and miscommunication. If you're over the age of 11, you probably know what most of these games are because it's in the preteen stage that we all begin to discover our sexual selves. And in a lot of homes, parents think that we don't have a good understanding about sex, so instead of talking to us about the "big act", they ignore the issue entirely until we come home pregnant or brokenhearted. So let's begin by clearing up some myths and defining the games that we play.

TOUCH ME, TEASE ME

At some point on this journey, we all reach a place where we decide to test the limits of our abstinence to see just how far we can go without actually "doing it" (and we all know what "it" is). So in this quest to find our boundaries, we often engage in the game of Tease. The rules for this game go a little like this: I make him think he can get more than I actually plan to give.

Adolescent Games

If you're in Middle School and Jr. High, your scenario may sound a little like this:

I smile at him (Jay) and he knows I like him. I wink my eye and he winks back. He really likes me. I pass him a note in class or instant message his best friend to see if Jay likes me. His friend says that he likes me, so we go to the movies. I tell my mom that I'm going to the Friday night movie with Ashley, but I secretly meet him there and we sit together. Our hands touch when we both reach for the popcorn. I think I saw fireworks in the sky. We hold hands. It's now the middle of the movie and his hand is on my leg. This is so cool, but I'm gonna make him stop before he gets to my panties. Wait until I tell Ashley!

Teen Games

This is the beginning of a lifetime of playing the Tease game. If you're in high school, this scenario may sound a little more familiar:

He's so cute. I'm gonna let him get to second base, light petting. I smile at him after football practice, and I get his phone number to call him later that evening. I call him on his cell and ask him if he wants to go to the movies this Friday. I don't know what the movie is about because we kiss throughout the movie. We stop by McDonald's with our friends, then Jay and I go parking. He thinks he's going to make it to home base, but I don't want it to go that far. But since I'm in the mood for some light petting, I'll just stop him when we get to that point. I may even let him give me a hickey...wait until I tell Ashley!

Both of these scenarios are alarming because they happen everyday. There's so much that's wrong with the above pictures, so let's take a look at them. In the first scenario, SHE takes interest in a guy and expresses it to his friend, instead of the other way around. So after "chasing" him, she decides before they even meet at the movies that she's going to let him feel her up so that she can tell her friend, but she really has no intention of going any further. So she basically responds in a way that makes him think one thing when she has already predetermined that her actions will be something entirely different. And we won't even discuss the small untruth — also known as a LIE — that she tells her mother!

In the second scenario, girlfriend is so on her own program. She schemes to get a date, putting herself out there to potentially get her feelings hurt, then follows through on her desire to get touched, but not go all the way. So she makes him think that he's gonna get some, but she knows all along that it's just a game…NO wonder guys are so confused by the time they make it to college. They've been exposed to the game since middle school! Ladies, if we know that we aren't planning to go all the way THERE, why fake it? Why lead a guy on to get our small perks when we know that they're thinking Grand Slam and we're thinking more along the lines of pop-up or incomplete play? Is there any fairness in this situation?

Yes, we all have our needs. You want to feel his hands there because, quietly, it's a pretty good feeling. And it doesn't hurt that you can tell your friends about it later. But when we play this game, we become participants in ruining the basic trust that men and women have in each other. Once men become hip to the game, how long do you think it will take before they begin playing their version of the game — to *hit it* at all costs (excluding rape, which is NEVER an option)? Only now the stakes are higher — you toyed with his physical attraction to you; the older guy, who's now wiser to the game, will toy with your emotions. So when you stop to think about it, the TEASE game really isn't all that it's cracked up to be. If you're planning to explore your sexuality, which I do not advocate, then at least be honest with the guy instead of stringing him along when you KNOW you're still maintaining your Virginity at all costs!

PETTING & ORAL SEX

Petting

This is probably the most detrimental game out there. The reason I believe Petting to be one of the most detrimental games is because it's the final step before sex. I like to compare it to marijuana. Many experts believe that weed is the gateway drug to crack and ecstasy; once a person reaches the weed high, she easily makes her way to the next high, often times in the form of X (ecstasy) or Crack. And once the more potent drugs are used, most users become addicted, which leads to other issues like disease, poverty, crime and violence. In many ways, petting is weed. It's the gateway drug to sex. And once you become sexually active, it's much more difficult to stop than to just never start at all. Right about now you're probably wondering what makes me the expert on this subject since I've obviously not had sex before. Well the answer to that question lies in the lives of many of my friends who have always been very open with me about the subject.

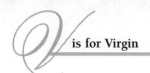

One story that I'd like to share with you is that of my friend Tamika* (name changed for anonymity) who kept her virginity until she graduated from college. At the ripe old age of 22, she decided that petting was no longer enough of a high, so she moved up to oral sex — known by its technical name as cunnilingus. And once that was no longer sufficient, she took the plunge into sex, with penal penetration. Regret. Confusion. Pain. All the side-effects of the act. And guess what? She didn't even enjoy it for the first several times! But what was there left for her to do after sex? Nothing. That's the glass ceiling on the high. So when you're sitting or lying there thinking that petting is the best invention next to sliced bread and the Sidekick pager, just remember that when you blow your high, there's only one more option left…Now do you think it's worth it?

Oral Sex — The New French Kiss

For some reason I cannot fully understand, many teens and pre-teens are under the impression that oral sex is basically the same as a kiss. I asked some teens what they thought about giving and receiving these type "favors", and the remarks I received are surprising. Many of the guys said that oral sex is something they expect to receive as part of their relationship with their girlfriend, although it is acceptable to have this sex act performed by someone they just know from school who isn't their girlfriend. HOWEVER, the common response is that they would not perform oral sex on a girl who wasn't their girlfriend. Girls, on the other hand, had no problem giving oral sex to someone who wasn't their boyfriend, and didn't expect the guy to return the favor. Some girls said that they don't really like to perform oral sex, but they want the guys to like them, or they want to be popular. I also found that these teens didn't believe that there was much of a chance of getting an STD, so like kissing, oral sex is relatively safe.

Hmmm...To this I say, "Oral Sex is Sex". Your body is still being used to bring a certain pleasure that God ordained for marriage. Rationalizing this act as something other than what it is doesn't change the fact that it's sex...so all of the same rules apply.

TEST DRIVE

Another game that is quite popular these days is the Test Drive. When a person buys a car, she test-drives it to make sure it rides smoothly over bumps as well as over smooth terrain. She checks the air conditioner and the sound system. She examines the seats and every now and then she checks the mileage. And the very first thing she notices is the body shape, style and color. Often times we interchange our theory on car buying with that of choosing a mate. I am constantly asked the questions "So how are you not going to have sex with a man before you marry him?" "What if he's no good in bed?" "You're a smart girl. You wouldn't buy a car without test-driving, so how can you justify choosing a mate without trying him out first?" To say I'd be rich if I had a dollar for every time a person asked me that question is a grave understatement.

So the following is my homemade analysis of the TEST DRIVE:

Smooth Ride: The average person tests the smoothness of a car to make sure that it rides well over various terrain. These people have suggested to me that I should do the same thing sexually with my partner, but I've taken a different approach to the test. I believe that a relationship is sooooo much more than sex, so I want to know how he rides in a relationship. How does he treat people when they are on his last nerve? Is he compassionate towards children, the elderly, and his family? Is he supportive when I'm having a bad day or when I decide to transfer schools or change careers? How does he act on my good days? What's his behavior on HIS bad days? Does he encourage my dreams? Does he love my inner qualities, since it's inevitable that my outer qualities won't be the same in 50 years? These are questions for a long road trip that cannot be answered with a roll in the hay.

Air & Sound: When deciding on a car, the accessories can make or break the deal. A car without air or a CD player may bring in far less than a fully loaded edition. This information is great, you say, but how does it relate to sex? Well, some may equate these accessories to a man's sexual creativity. Does he add spice to the bedroom drama? Are there tricks in his magic hat? This line of questioning takes me to a different place. When I think of the accessories, I'm more concerned with his creativity five or ten years from now. When our time is spread thin because of jobs and kids and "married stuff," will his creative juices flow in the direction of spicing up our lives? Will he still remember the important days of the year, like my birthday and our first kiss? Will he hide notes for me in special places where I'll be delightfully surprised to find them? For me, the long-haul answers are far more important than any trick he might pull out of a sex bag (not that I won't expect those treats after we're married!).

Seats: Oh my goodness! These days there are sooooo many options on the seats of a car! Someone taking a test-drive may be overwhelmed by the gadgets that custom fit the chair to the driver. There's back movement and bottom movement. And don't forget the heated seats, all in the name of comfort. Now some of my friends who question my choice of abstinence may be interested in the physical comfort of two melding bodies, and that's their thing. But for me, I'm more concerned with a relational fit. Comfort and compatibility for me have more to do with us being spiritually in line than with us lining up toe to toe in bed. Do we get along well together? Does he cover me in prayer, and do I cover him? Can we go for days without talking, but then, like the custom seats, automatically readjust without skipping a beat? That's the comfort that's most important for building a strong relationship that will last.

Mileage: OK, here's a biggie when test-driving. If there was a choice given to a buyer where one car had less miles than the other, I believe we'd all jump at the one less driven for all sorts of reasons, starting with less wear and tear on the car. I think that the same can be said for men choosing women, but with women choosing men, it seems that the more popular choice is the more experienced man. And why would that be the case? Probably because society reinforces the "experienced man" ideal. I think men would prefer a less seasoned woman, but women are just different.

Even as far back as high school, I recall the most popular, advanced guys being the most sought after. With my maturity, I've come to the conclusion that more mileage is not such a good thing. The more exposed a person is to sex, the higher the probability that he has been affected by disease. One of my friends explained to me that human papilloma virus (see chapter 8) is one that's carried in one of three sexually active people. So if you have sex with someone who has had sex with at least two other people, you become part of the statistic. And while this disease won't kill you, I hear it's aggravating as hell. So sometimes less mileage is actually better. (and let's not forget the baggage that comes with mileage — see chapter 5)

Body Shape, Style, Color: Before a test-drive even begins, some of the more important factors have already been taken into consideration on sight alone. The shape, style and color are very important to a buyer, but in terms of choosing a man or having sex with him, these attributes may be observed from a different perspective. Some would say that physical attraction is the end all and be all of sex, but since I believe that sex is more mental than physical, I take a somewhat different approach to the aesthetics. Now that's not to say that attraction means nothing because I'm the LAST person trying to be with a *booga,* but I think there's more to this synopsis than meets the eye. Yes it's great to have someone who's buff, but for me, a tight physique means that he takes care of his temple. He finds time in his busy day to take care of what God has given him, which let's me know that it's very likely that he will take care of me! With style and color, I think more in terms of sense of self and personality. For me, a nice physique, warm personality and secure sense of self is probably great for sex, but more importantly, these attributes will spill over into all aspects of his life. So when asked if I think it's a good idea to skip the test drive, I believe that a test drive for specific reasons is needed, but not for sex. I once heard author/speaker P. Bunny Wilson say that sex is a teachable act, as long as the partner is willing and physically able…so cheers to the suspense and the wait!

COMMUNICATION

The final game of which you should be aware is the Communication G.A.P. (gaming and playing). This game is almost like cat and mouse: "What he says, What he means, What you hear". I've found over the years that the communication between men and women is not as complex as we would have it be. The books and classes teach that men and women have different thinking patterns. I believe that's true, but I also believe that for the most part, women understand much (albeit not all) of what men mean, but we play a game to make things end the way we want them to end.

It amuses me to no end to watch women manipulate men by pretending not to know what's up. If a guy says he's not ready for commitment, but you go ahead and have sex with him, telling him that you're cool with it, you're gaming. **He said:** I don't want a commitment. **He meant:** I don't want a commitment. **You Heard:** He doesn't want to commit to me, so I'll have sex with him, knowing that I love him, and then he'll love me back and want to commit to me and if that doesn't work, I'll have a baby. Baby girl, **You heard him, but what you really heard was yourself!** Hence the GAME as we know it. And granted, sometimes there really is some misunderstanding just because men and women communicate differently, but please know that when a guy says something like "no commitment", no amount of bootie from you is going to change that. But what WILL happen is more baggage for you! (see chapt. 5). Game Over.

Now that you have been schooled in the GAME, we're gonna move on to the RULES of the GAME in the next chapter. These rules will teach you how to avoid the G.A.P. and embrace a new game — a new lifestyle. But before that, please take the next few minutes to answer the questions on the following page just to make sure you clearly understand the message of this chapter.

Questions

1 What are the five ways that the GAME is manifested?

1) __________

2) __________

3) __________

4) __________

5) __________

2 Reflecting on your past relationships, how do *you* typically play the game?

3 How can you modify your actions and thoughts to maintain your goal of abstinence?

CHAPTER TWO

The Rules: How to Effectively Abstain

Ok, we've just learned all about the games that we play, so let's take a moment to review the rules of the game. Just like any board game that you may play, there are also guidelines to govern the activity and help you win the challenge of Abstinence. People are always amazed when they learn that I'm still a virgin in my post-collegiate life. I think one of the main reasons this fact comes as a surprise to them is because I don't look or act like anything they may associate with a sex-free lifestyle. I've always been popular, being voted "Most Likely to Succeed" and serving as Senior Class president in high school. I enjoy wearing the latest fashions, although I usually add my personal style to my outfits. Throughout high school and college, I participated in student government and other extra curricular activities, being voted 2nd Attendant to Miss Spelman at my alma mater. I pledged a sorority in my sophomore year, where I spent much of my time participating in community service projects. And I also worked a part time job fundraising on campus, where I was afforded the opportunity to meet alumnae and corporate sponsors from all walks of life. Moreover at the ripe young age of 25, I purchased my first home and served as director for a celebrity charity. So from the looks of things, there's nothing dramatically different from me and any other person my age, except the sex factor. So when I hear the tales of how impossible it is for one to remain a virgin, withstanding peer pressure yet still being cool, I can't believe the hype. When it all boils down to it, abstinence is far from easy, but it is NOT AN IMPOSSIBILITY!

So, here are a few of the rules that I use to help me maintain in this game.

Don't put yourself in compromising situations: It boggles my mind when I hear stories from young ladies who say, "it just happened". Life does not "just happen" like that without some effort on our part. We are living creatures who have the gift of choice. Sometimes our decisions are good and sometimes they're not so good, but the choice is definitely ours to make. So why on earth do we find ourselves in positions where "it just happened"? Deut. 30:19 states that in choosing between blessings and cursing that are set before us, we should choose life! I believe we find ourselves in these *iffy* positions because we CHOSE to be there. Why else are you in the back of his Escalade or between his sheets? Did someone blindfold and handcuff you? If so, you have been kidnapped and should file a report with your local law enforcement agency. If this is not your situation, then you're there because you decided that "there" is where you wanted to be.

During my college years, I'd sometimes find myself in very compromising situations, but it was because I decided to stop by *his* house with *him* after a movie, knowing that *he* lived an hour from campus, which would inevitably mean an overnight stay (or some other equally not-so-bright scenario). And how on earth did I plan to spend the night and not risk having something happen that shouldn't? I never gave it much thought because in my youth, some of my foolish decisions were just that — foolish!

Flee Temptation: The bible says "resist the devil and he will flee", (James 4:7) a scripture that many of us use to help us in our walk. If we yield not to temptation, it will inevitably go away. For example, if I tell this fine, Tyson look-a-like that I'm not trying to have sex with him, he'll go away. Well, yes he probably will, but why even take the risk of being in the situation where anything like sex will pop off?

Two scriptures that I prefer to lean on state that I should "flee sexual temptation" {(ii tim 2:22) "flee youthful lusts…" & (1 cor 6:18) "flee fornication. Every sin that a man does is without the body; but he that commits fornication sins against his own body"}. It's such a wiser choice to just flee the temptation all together. Now I'm not saying that we should run from challenges or not be bold and walk in kingdom authority where satan is concerned. What I AM saying is that it makes soooo much sense to just RUN from the situation BEFORE it becomes a compromising one. Like when you're making out on the sofa or wherever and the little voice inside is telling you to stop while you're ahead, maybe instead of sitting (or lying, which is more probable) there, just leave — you don't even have to pray about it. It sounds so complex, but it really isn't. Yes, he's fine as all get out — maybe a cross between Tyrese and Allen Iverson, with Usher's dimple and smile. Um um um…anyway, you're in a compromising situation already, so why sit there and try to rationalize with yourself why it's ok that you are where you are when you can clearly hear yourself telling yourself to get up and leave! Just flee! You'll feel much better about things the next day when your heart and your hymen are both in tact. And in case of emergency, just call Jesus really loudly. This act is sure to stop the presses!

Pray to be Kept: There's a song "O, To Be Kept By Jesus" that older saints in my church used to sing. This song became my anthem for several years. Let me just tell you that when you pray and ask Him to keep you, which means to help you in your pursuit of abstinence, He will do just that. I kid you not, there have been a couple times when, feeling that I was grown enough to do the grown-up, I decided to take the plunge. I mean really, when you're 22 knocking on 23, it's like "ok God, thanks for the good times, but I'm out!" So when I reached this milestone, I decided that I wanted to know what the hype was all about. Since it didn't seem like I would be getting married anytime soon, I decided to make my own moves.

I picked up a Victoria's Secret catalogue and chose the cutest little number I could find, something that was knee-length because I still wasn't trying to look like a stripper or anything. Unbeknownst to my poor victim, I had made all the necessary arrangements for an intimate evening that I thought would revolutionize my life. I consulted with my sex counselor (my roommate at the time) to find out what I needed to do to make sure that my mission was accomplished, and all that was left to do was to pick him up from the airport that evening. Well I'm sure you can imagine my surprise when I get to the airport and find an unexpected sorority sister waiting for me to pick her up. To this day I DO NOT know why she was there or how she knew that I would be at the airport, but I have a sneaky suspicion that God had something to do with it. Even when I wanted to have sex, He kept me, just like he keeps all of his other promises. And now when I think on it, that wasn't the first time God sabotaged my plans. On the other occasions, He always managed to fix the guy's heart to encourage me in my path for abstinence. Go figure. What joy. Can you just imagine having the Lord break up your personal party? Ask and He'll do the same for you!

Know Your Limitations: Nobody knows you better than you know you, so in this game it's imperative that you are aware of your limitations. If you know that holding hands and kissing is cool for you, then hey, that's your thing, but if a little tongue makes you feel tingly like you want to be naked, then you should know that this is your limit. Take a timeout, girl! Don't wait "just a little longer" or "10 more seconds 'cause this feels good". STOP while you're ahead. Just let it go.

Because we are all individuals, we all have different breaking points, which is why it's so imperative that you know your own. It's so easy for younger ladies to try to gauge their own limitations by what their girlfriend has told them about hers. But this situation can only turn out for the worst because if your girl's limit before she wants to have sex is having a guy kiss her neck and yours is having a guy kiss your lips, guess who's going to pass her point of no return when he moves from the lips to the neck? YOU, silly! So it's of the utmost importance that you know when to say when.

A couple of tricks that I've used to help me with this type situation is to create diversions which give me just enough time to get out of compromising situations. One such diversion, not shaving my legs, is one that I freely pass on to all of you, while the other is one that I'll tell you about as a bit of a confession and to help you not make the same mistakes that I've made. I once heard on T.V. or somewhere that the best way to ensure that I not have sex on a date is by not shaving my legs. Most women are particular about hair on their legs, although I have friends who are comfortable with never shaving. But for the majority of us who do shave, it would be a sin and a crime for a love interest to see or touch our hairy legs. This notion turns out to be by far the cheapest and most effective form of sex-control that I've found to date! So when I know that I'm going on a date, I simply let the hairs on my legs grow and I NEVER have a problem going any further than hand-holding and maybe a kiss.

The second method, one that I DO NOT advise, is what I call the *fat factor.* I have found over the years that when my weight is lower, I'm pursued by men all of the time, but when I'm thicker, the date requests sharply decline. So with that in mind, it has been much easier for me to maintain my virginity because I've narrowed down the chances in my favor. However, I'm quick to let you know that this is NOT a good idea. I have found that while the *fat factor* deters dinner invitations, it doesn't do a whole lot for my self-image or self-esteem. So I'm currently trying to handle the whole mindset that comes along with the *fat factor.* And in monitoring my other virgin friends, I've found similar characteristics. The *fat factor* has become a shield or a type of male-repellent which allows us to be the wonderful people we are without having to deal much with unwanted, and sometimes wanted, overtures from men. Sometimes the *fat factor* surfaces in the form of weight, but I've also seen it camouflaged with clothing that give the appearance of weight that's not really there. I have one friend who insists on wearing oversized clothes for just this reason. She's a beautiful, intelligent doctor who hides behind a size 12 when she's really more like a size 8. I have another friend who pushes her obesity on the back burner because the weight offers a certain level of comfort for her; the weight allows her the security of knowing that she will probably never be pulled out of the crowd as "the one", so her virginity is still in tact. After studying this phenomenon, I've come to the conclusion that virginity is great, but it shouldn't consume one's personality to the point where she hides her true self from the world. So in recognizing your limitations, be sure that you don't resort to unhealthy tactics to help you on this journey.

Know Your Ovulation Cycle and STAY HOME!!!: Oh my goodness. This is one of the most important rules to playing the game. Bunny Wilson, one of my favorite "singles" experts, spoke at my church in Atlanta and of all the wonderful information she dropped, I believe that the lesson that most remained with me had everything to do with "timing". Bunny gave a breakdown of the menstruation cycle and ovulation period, which basically shows the peak time for the highest estrogen level (see chapter 3). This time is usually within a 10-day window before a woman receives her period, and it's a time when a woman's body is ready to conceive a child.

Because the estrogen level is so high, the body goes through somewhat of a craving frenzy. During this time, your body is literally CRAVING sex and there's nothing that you can do to stop this process. So the best advice that can be given is this: during that time of the month, right before your period, STAY HOME!!! Even when you have the best of intentions, when your mind is focused and your heart is pure, this phenomenon will take place. So please don't feel like you're a freak or whatever because of these physical feelings. I remember, before I heard this hormonal explanation, I would feel so bad about once a month. I felt just awful, like I was the biggest slut walking — not because I'd done anything, but because my body was waging a war with my mind, encouraging, no — demanding, that I have sex! So I was definitely relieved when I spent some time learning more about my body and my cycle. Now on those days, which sometimes vary between 3 and 5 days each month, I cuddle up to a book or a movie or, when it's really bad, a nice pint of Chocolate Chip Cookie Dough.

Surround Yourself With Encouraging Friends: In anything that you do, it's important to have supportive angels in your corner. This idea is a maker-and-breaker for someone trying to maintain her virginity. Most of my friends are sexually active, but they are sooo supportive of my choice to abstain from sex until marriage. Even in those times when I decided that enough was enough, some of my friends would catch wind of my decisions and immediately e-mail or call me to harass me about saving my body until the right time.

Over the years I've found that true friends only want what's best for you and they will move heaven and earth to try to make sure you get the best. It's really interesting to see how overprotective my friends have become with time. They all act like mother hens and give my dates the third, fourth and fifth degree to make sure that my best interest is fully in focus. Sometimes this can be a pain in the butt, but at least I can never question the love my true friends have for me. So, having this type support makes a virgin's life much easier. They are so full of information and go to great lengths to make sure I know EVERYTHING...from the specifics on STDs to the emotional problems associated with sex. Our conversations aren't always doom and gloom because they also make sure that I understand as well as I can what sex is about. So it's almost like having the best of both worlds…almost.

It's also great to have friends who, too, are virgins with whom you can relate and discuss life. For years I thought I was one of only maybe two virgins, and I figured the other one lived on Mars or somewhere else without the modern technology of the 2-way. In college, however, I realized that there are many women making the decision to abstain, but *we* aren't shown on the music videos, sitcoms, or magazines that are mainstream.

Reinforce Your Choices With Scripture: The ultimate rule to winning this game of abstinence is keeping the Word of God somewhere in your face so that you will have a cushion when you fall. There will be times when controlling your mind from lustful thoughts or simple pleasure fantasies is an impossible task to do. It's at these times that you can look up on the wall or on your bathroom mirror or your car dashboard to reaffirm your decision to abstain. It will seem elementary at best, but placing reminders in places where you see them daily will help keep you encouraged to play by ALL the rules and ultimately win the game! People are quick to quote Proverbs 31, the story of the virtuous woman, but this account of a perfect woman really seems to elude most of us. Now this isn't to say that there's anything wrong with trying to be a perfect woman, but sometimes this scripture just seems impossible and rather unrealistic. So for those who are not encouraged by this often-used text, there are others on which you can meditate. Some of my favorite lifelines are:

> *"All things work together for the good of them who love the Lord and are called according to His purpose"* (Rom 8:28)

> *"I can do all things through Christ who strengthens me"* (Phil 4:13)

> *"And the Peace of God, which passes all understanding, shall keep your heart and mind through Christ Jesus"* (Phil 4:7)

> *"Now unto him that is able to keep you from falling and present you faultless before the presence of his Glory with exceeding joy, to the only wise God our Savior, be glory and majesty, dominion and power, both now and forever. Amen"* (Jude 1:24-25)

So my friend, you are now equipped to take on the ultimate challenge. Since you know the games and possess the rules for the *ultimate challenge*, let's now take a few steps back to gain a broader perspective of the physiological aspect of SEX.

Questions

1 **What are the rules for abstinence?**

2 **Why is it important to know the changes in your cycle?**

3 **Why is it important to have peer support?**

CHAPTER 3

Anatomy 101

For a long time, I used to think that something was wrong with me because every month around the same time my body would start giving me *fits* — that's what I call that irrepressible urge to have sex. Like I said before, I was raised in a Pentecostal church, so this feeling was NOT at all acceptable. Being too ashamed or embarrassed to ask anyone what was happening with my body, or maybe just ignorant, I kept the secret to myself and suffered alone. It never even dawned on me that maybe, just maybe other people caught *fits* too. I guess I thought that only fast girls had to deal with being horny. And it wasn't until I was in my mid 20's that I learned about the biological reasons I felt the way I did.

There are a couple of things that happen to us biologically that make our bodies crave sex: 1) increased estrogen during the menstruation cycle and 2) production of dopamine (a pleasure chemical released in the brain). Both of these affect the way our bodies process the need for sex.

INCREASED ESTROGEN DURING THE MENSTRUATION CYCLE

During a woman's menstruation cycle, or period, there are usually four weeks that you are working with. In the first week (which is actually the end of your period), your ovaries release a follicle that begins to release estrogen. In the second week, this release of estrogen increases to a high level that actually causes a communication with the hypothalamus (part of the brain) that makes you crave sex. The second week, the mid point of the cycle, also stimulates the release of two other chemicals (*FSH* — follicle stimulating hormone and *LH* — luteinizing hormone) from the pituitary gland in the brain. {NOTE: sex hormones enhance sensations, which activate sexual behavior}. In the third week, the follicle releases its ovum (which is what we refer to as the egg) which, in the fourth week, is either discarded during your period or fertilized with sperm. The sac that once held the egg now produces progesterone, which when combined a week later with estrogen, greatly enhances the biological desire for sex.

Now this sounds a little complex, but I really wanted to give you a scientific explanation for the feelings that you are sure to have about two weeks before your period. In more simple terms, your body tries to produce a child once each month. The ovaries releasing an egg that can either be fertilized by your man OR expunged from your body during your flow do this. Because of all the build up of hormones (or estrogens that enlarge the area of skin that excites the nerve which transmits stimulation from the pubic area to the brain), you will always be more sensitive about mid-way through the 30 day cycle. It's at these times that you might want to take up a hobby to occupy yourself so that you don't let your body make decisions for your mind, heart and soul.

THE EFFECTS OF DOPAMINE

Some medical experts define dopamine as a pleasure chemical that's released in the body to turn you on or sexually stimulate you. Others disagree. So when I began to research the particulars of the sex chemical, as it is often called, I had to rely on some of my doctor-girlfriends. The consensus is as follows: There is a part of our brain in the hypothalamus portion called the medial preoptic area (MPOA). This particular area is one of the main ones affected by the sex hormones. These hormones influence the brain, particularly the MPOA, to release dopamine. When dopamine is released in moderate quantities, the result tends to be a high level of arousal in women, but when it's released in larger quantities, the result stimulates orgasms. During the second week of a woman's cycle, the time where both estrogen and progesterone meet, the combination becomes the most effective stimulation for sexual behavior in women. So during this particular phase of the cycle, you may want to post a "BEWARE" sign on your mirror as a reminder of your fragile state, since we all know that sometimes mind over matter is not enough.

I hope that this information sheds some light on what is really going on with your body. It's so unfortunate that there aren't many, if any, resources readily available to offer guidance and just plain ol' information on something so basic as our hormonal process. I wish that I had known the details of how my body works years ago because I would have been more comfortable with my situation. I would have known how to count the days leading up to my *fits*, and prepare myself for the inevitable battle with my body, instead of always being side-swiped, and then thinking that something was wrong with me. I've included a sample calendar on the next page that you can use to help you chart your cycle until you're able to recognize the signs for yourself. I hope this helps!

Sample "Warning" Calendar

(10 – 14 DAYS BEFORE PERIOD)

		1	2	3	4	5
6 warning...	7 warning...	8 warning...	9 warning...	10 warning...	11 warning...	12 warning...
13 warning...	14 warning...	15 warning...	16 warning...	17 warning...	18 warning...	19 warning...
20 PERIOD	21	22	23	24	25	26
27	28	29	30	31		

Questions

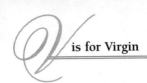

1 **How does estrogen effect the body's need for sex?**

____

____

____

2 **What effect does dopamine have on the body during the monthly cycle?**

____

____

____

3 **At what point in the menstruation cycle is the estrogen level at its peak?**

____

____

____

For more information on the biological aspect of sex, please reference the following:

- Baron, Robert A. and Donn Byrne. *Social Psychology,* 9th ed. Allyn and Bacon, Boston, 2000. Chapter 11, pp 334-339.
- Kalat, James W. *Biological Psychology,* 7th ed. Wadsworth, USA, 2001. Chapter 11, pp 312-319.

CHAPTER 4

Guarding Your Mind

"Finally brethren, whatsoever things are true,
whatsoever things are honest,
whatsoever things are just,
whatsoever things are pure,
whatsoever things are lovely,
whatsoever things are of good report;
if there be any virtue, and if there be any praise,
think on these things"

(Philippians 4:8)

MUSIC

Not too long ago in church, my pastor made a comment that almost blew my mind. His divine revelation from God dealt with what happens to the mind when the body sleeps and compared it to the Holy Spirit when the body functions on automatic in our daily lives. He said that the fal things we think about before bed remain on our minds while we sleep and when we awake the next morning. So I guess that's why I can go to bed thinking about the assignments and to do lists for the next day and wake up dead tired! And the same is what happens to our spirits throughout the day, while we go through our routines. The music that we listen to, or the conversations that we have remain in our spirits while we're on automatic pilot, which brings us to this question: What ARE you thinking?!!!

My job is located about 45 minutes from my house, so I flip radio stations on my way to the office. Because the Gospel radio stations don't consistently play the urban-type contemporary songs that I like, I tend to flip between the Hip Hop, R&B, Pop, and Old School stations. So one day this summer, as I took my lengthy trek to work, I heard this song with a really hot beat, and before I knew it, I was singing all the words and really just feelin' this song. Since this song was so popular, I could flip stations all day long and find it everywhere. Meanwhile in my real life, I found that I was becoming anxious to find a mate, which usually was not such a huge issue. And it never dawned on me that perhaps my repeated chanting of Missy Elliot's "Get Your Freak On" may have had something to do with my state of mind… until I received

God's message about guarding my mind.

I realized several years ago that certain songs evoke certain feelings, but since I hate when "super-deep" Christians harp on secular music, I just kind of took the issue with a grain of salt. I mean, really, who wants to exist in a life without music? Being a Christian shouldn't mean that a person has to give up music…this has always been my train of thought. So my solution was to simply turn the station when feeling-evoking songs came on. And this has always worked just fine for me…but what happens when you become attached to the music of a song and don't really pay attention to the words? Well, those words sink into your mind and that becomes what you meditate on. I know from experience (since I deal with the music issue daily) that meditating on topics that do not assist you in your decision for abstinence only makes things harder.

I'm not suggesting that you stop listening to secular music because I think that music directs our culture, so it's imperative that we keep in touch with what's going on in the world, but I DO suggest that we take more precautions in guarding what enters our mind. So IF a "sexsexsexandmoresex" song should be playing on your radio, be conscious enough to either turn the station or turn the station, because the last thing any of us needs is sexual encouragement laid on top of tight beats!

MAGAZINES & BOOKS

Whew, this is a big one too. Music is really a strong tool for suggestion, but visual stimulus is stronger. When I stand in the line at the grocery store, two things jump out at me. The first is that most of the women on the covers of the mags are scantily clad, if they're dressed at all. The second thing that screams at me is the titles and subtitles. Have you ever just taken a second to read the covers of these magazines? They range from "1001 Ways to Improve Your Sex Life" to "1001 new Kama Sutra Moves and More!!!". And then the clincher is the one article that is really of any substance that catches the attention of even the most diligent virgin: "Fashion Trends On A Budget"! Now who can pass this magazine without buying it? And now, within an hour's time, your interest in next season's fashions leads you down a path of questionnaires, quizzes and sex notes…

It's hilarious to me the creativity that some of these magazines use, in the form of a layout, that catch us completely off guard. First there's the special interest story: Your favorite singer goes on vacation in the Mediterranean and takes her MAC Lip Glass with her as the only provision she can't live without…Cool, no damage done. Then there are the pictures of some of next season's hottest accessories, with the value-priced editions on the next page…We're still cool so far. And then it appears — the Interactive Survey where 5 men are asked about which dresses make the "models" look crazy/sexy/cool. In one fell swoop, it's done! Now we're entranced in a world of "does he think THIS is sexy? I should get something like that"…Next page, 1001 Ways to Please Your Mate by Adding Spice to your Sex Life…and you're still reading (possibly justifying it with "well, I can use this tidbit when I'm married"). This simple act of reading without really filtering the information now has you in the mall searching for "that" dress that 4 of the 5 guys thought was sexy. So here you are, dwelling on topics that do not assist you on your road to maintaining abstinence. Guarding your mind is an act that you can't just overlook or do "sometimes".

For the longest time, I wondered about these type magazines and whether or not I would ever find some current reading material that still discussed relationship issues, fashion, and careers that didn't include the *sex factor.* And it wasn't until this year that I realized I'm not the only one in search of this type periodical — one that won't interfere with what I feed my mind...So if something just leaped inside of you when you read this, take that as a sign to step out and provide the magazine that has such a need right now.

And speaking of reading books, another form of entertainment that I have had to break a hold from is much of the African American fictional novels. I'm not suggesting that anything is wrong with these books; I actually find many of them to be quite enjoyable. Reading them, for me, became an issue when I read before bed, went to sleep, and awoke with the same passionate scene in my mind...only usually transforming the faces into mine and the object of my affections. Because of my love of reading, I could sit and read them one after the next, never getting enough of the stories, but what good were these books for my spirit and my walk of abstinence? None...enough said.

MTV

As I write this book, MTV is celebrating its 20th Anniversary. For the past 2 decades, nearly all my life, this mode of media (the combination of visual and audio) has brought all sorts of immorality into our homes. And please note, this is not a suggestion that censorship occur or anything like that, but it's simply the stating of facts. My first real recollection of the station centers around the Michael Jackson "Billie Jean" video. Before I ever listened to the album, I was visually introduced to premarital sex in a popular and seemingly positive way.

Because I was born out of wedlock, I have always been keenly aware of fornication, one reason my decision for abstinence is so real for me. However, premarital sex was never ever glorified in my home or community. So with the "Billie Jean" video, I became aware of another view on premarital sex. To summarize the song, MJ croons that he's not the father of a child who is obviously born to someone with whom he had sex, but didn't love. He then dances on the sidewalk, which lights up with each step he takes. Validation by such a musical icon could have definitely swayed an impressionable young woman in the direction of premarital sex because, through MTV and other music video shows, the video supported the notion that public opinion was comfortable with the *sex factor.*

Over time, the fashion has changed and the vj's have been traded, but the heart of the music video industry has remained constant in walking the fine line of what society will tolerate and pushing the envelope further. Now, some

20 year's later, the *sex factor* has evolved from just lyrical content to lyrics with visual aids. If a song talks about being a "baby's daddy", there probably exists a scene in the video which shows the "conception"...also known as sex. There was one video that I watched that talked in-depth about oral sex and actually showed the acts slightly veiled, but still quite revealing.

Since images are so strong, not only are the affected generations becoming younger and younger, but those of us who are running the race of abstinence are finding it harder and harder to just maintain. And more than that, with these images constantly in your mind, just hearing the song on the radio is reinforced by the visuals you've seen in the videos. So guarding your mind becomes more of a task each day, but letting any and every image into your mind and spirit is not an option if you plan to succeed at this game.

CONVERSATIONS

A final note of caution for guarding your mind: be careful of the conversations that you have. You can't just talk to anyone about everything. For some people, having a discussion about all the positions they've tried and the sex toys they've purchased does not really affect their state of mind, mainly because they are not in a place where abstinence is an option that they're choosing. However, a person who is trying to refrain from trying out "positions" or "toys" is likely to have a seed planted that will take far more energy to erase than it would have to have simply avoided the conversation completely. Once the conversation takes place, there's now room for curiosity of the mind. Such curiosity inevitably leads to sinful thoughts…so why even go there?

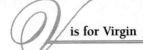

Now that you have been made aware of some of the larger issues that can attack your mind, you should be better equipped to attack them. I suggest that you post the scriptures given in this chapter all throughout your home/car/office and refer to them as needed, which is DAILY.

Questions

1 How is the Holy Spirit living in you affected by what you see, hear, and do?

____

____

____

2 In what way does music affect us on a subconscious level?

____

____

____

3 List three practical activities that you will use to filter the images that you see and hear in the media.

1) ____

____

2) ____

____

3) ____

____

CHAPTER 5

Guarding Your Heart

One of the most profound lessons that I ever learned had everything to do with protecting that which I never knew needed protection — my heart. "And the peace of God, which surpasses all understanding, shall guard your heart and mind through Christ Jesus" (Phil 4:7). You know, I've always been of the opinion that we, as human beings, would experience life in a fuller capacity if we would just open ourselves up to others, instead of living behind fences and walls, shielding ourselves from the potential of pain. It seems that we go through life wearing a saran wrap body bag, seeing what's going on, but not getting close enough to others to actually be touched or affected by them. So it is with this train of thought, of sharing my heart with others, that I existed…until I opened my heart to the wrong situation and circumstance.

You see, for a long time, I believed in the fairy tales of Prince Charming who would ride up in a white Escalade and take me away to a phat castle with an indoor swimming pool and basketball court. Hence, in my search for the Prince, I left my heart unguarded, open for any and everyone to trample over at will. In my ignorance, I shared too much too soon, which left me open for deeper, more painful wounds. In a matter of months, I had shared my inner most feelings with someone who I believed to be "the one". I had established a soul-ish relationship, or soul tie, which may never have happened had I not been "in search" for my prince. Scripture states that "he who finds a wife finds a good thing" (Prov 18:22), not the other way around.

A soul tie is a relationship that goes beyond the physical into the spiritual, creating a bond that unites individuals in possibly the strongest type relationship that exists. Many of the great theologians write that these bonds between men and women usually occur once sex has taken place, which is why, after a break up, the person may leave physically, but you are still very much attached to him. The other way that I have found this type bond to manifest is in the form of *conversational intimacy.* By this I mean that all the hours that you spend talking to "your boy" or someone who's "just a friend" eventually cross the line from "you know a little about me" to "you know almost EVERyTHIng about me. You must be the prince!" — a notion that may not give you the results you want. Just imagine — you share every dream and aspiration, painful past, hopeful future, aggravation, happiness, failure and success with this person, only to find that he's not trying to be with you...although you're his best friend on earth. And the only reason that this can happen is by not guarding your heart and not keeping some parts of yourself private until God sends you the person with whom you're supposed to share it.

It's very easy to slide into a space where you just want someone to talk to about your life — who you really are after you leave the public, what you really think when the camera turns off — the "unplugged" you. Wanting to share ourselves with another person is only natural, but knowing the limits of sharing is essential to guarding the most real part of who we are, our hearts. Now, I'm not suggesting that you close yourself off from people and walk around in a bubble. I'm saying that there should be a limit to what you share about yourself with another human being so as to avoid falling into the soul-tie trap. And the reason I say "falling" is because that's exactly what it is. I've never gone into a relationship saying that I wanted to share all my personal business with this person. If anything, I've probably said the exact opposite. I found that at the least expected time, I'd shared so much of who I am and been told so much about who he is that things just *felt* like a relationship. Now imagine the torturous feeling of trying to end this *soulish* relationship. Words cannot express the anguish and distress felt on both ends of the relationship, all because we shared too much too fast in a relationship that God did not ordain to be anything more than a friendship.

With male and female relationships, we have to be really careful not to cross the line. Since the painful dissolution of my soul-tie, I've learned a whole new way of communicating without letting the secret part of my heart become entangled. So do I still share some of my feelings with my boys? Yes, but not the emotions closest to my heart. Do I still discuss my hopes and dreams? Yes, but in a more broad, generic sense. I've learned how to walk the stress-line of having good friends who are male (platonic) without becoming attached to them the way one would with a boyfriend.

DADDY'S SUBSTITUTE

There exists another phenomenon regarding the heart that happens to a lot of young women today, stemming directly from issues that we have with our fathers. Many of us were not raised in two parent homes, and if we were, it's likely that the male figure was a stepfather or an emotionally "unavailable" dad. This absence of male attention left many of us starving for male affection and affirmation from whatever source we could find it. I truly believe that this search to quench our thirst for male validation has led many young ladies into the arms and beds of men, pushing the envelope on a letter that maybe we didn't want to read. If indeed a woman is called into who she is by her father, what happens when that paternal link is missing? We fall into the arms of sometimes well-intentioned men who tell us we're cute or smart or anything, as long as it's something. We are in search of an emotional fulfillment that is really just baggage that we carry with us from pillar to post.

For those of you who find yourself in this state, it is

most imperative that you guard your heart with dynamite or whatever it takes to keep YOU from being TAKEN. I know how it feels to just want to be around a man, whether it's just to hear a deep voice or to smell cologne like your friends' fathers wore or to get picked up and swung around and held like a baby. I know, ladies…and I also know that it's way too easy to confuse these emotions that may have been missing from your childhood with those from some guy you may be dating now.

As daughters, we have a huge space for our daddies. If in our childhoods these spaces are not filled, they shrink, but they never go away, which allows for another man to step into that spot later on in our lives. But please know that your boyfriend, future husband, or whatever can NEVER fill that space left by your father. Because we sometimes have difficulty differentiating the space of a missing dad from that of a new beau, we tend to offer more space to the boyfriend, just as a means of filling the gaping hole left by a missing father. Not only does this add baggage to any relationship, since the male now has to teeter the line between filling his space in your heart, as well as your father's, but it also opens you up to more pain because your capacity to hold the pain is bigger than that of another young lady without this set of issues. So it is of the utmost import that, for those who were not raised around your fathers, you realize what's up and make some adjustments to ensure that only an allotted space is up for grabs in the relationship war, with the first step being acknowledgement of the missing piece that created the space.

It's funny how God works. When I went through all the drama of my soul-tie, only a portion of which I've outlined here for you, I felt so empty inside. It wasn't a complete emptiness, but rather one where there was a hole just big enough for me to feel it (kinda like a small tooth cavity). One of the days when I felt my absolute worst, Father's Day 1998 I believe, I sat in church and listened as my pastor talked directly to women who had been raised by someone other than their biological fathers. As I sat there listening to all the effects of an absent father, I realized that many of them were directed to me. So I stood up with all the other young ladies and in my heart, I adopted my Spiritual Father as my dad.

I won't lie and say that the gaping hole in my heart closed up immediately, but over the next couple of years, I looked up and realized that the hole had become a much smaller issue. I say this to you to let you know that I feel where you are, and one of the ways that I dealt with the hole was by embracing my pastor as my father. Maybe this isn't the answer for everyone, but I promise that if you look and pray for a filling for the cavity in your heart, God will provide one for you!

In the last chapter, we reviewed how and why we should guard our minds at all times, making sure that we meditate on things that will help keep us on the path of virginity. In this chapter, I attempt to give a very real view of the effects of not guarding your heart. I also touch on one of the most painful subjects for many of us — *looking for daddy's love in all the wrong places.* I'd like for you to take a moment right now and think about your relationship with your father. Was he around? Even if you had a "substitute" dad, like an uncle or stepfather, was YOUR dad there for you emotionally, spiritually and financially? When you answer these questions, be real with yourself so that you can assess the size of the unfulfilled hole inside your heart and learn to guard it.

Questions

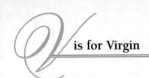

1 What is a soul-ish relationship?

2 Take a moment to evaluate your closest male female relationship. Have you crossed the line of friendship into soul-ties? If so, how can you effectively handle the situation?

3 Do you have a hole in your heart left by a missing father? If so, let's take a moment and ask God for a special touch.

Dear Father,

I stand before you, your daughter, acknowledging that there is an emptiness inside that I continue to try to fill without your help. The hole is empty because my father was not around to fill this particular void, so I tend to transfer the void onto other males who enter my life. Father, I don't want to always carry baggage into my relationships, and more than that, I don't want to continue to feel like a large part of me is missing. So I come to you now, acknowledging the gaping hole and asking that you fill it in a way that only you can. Please make me whole. In Jesus name I pray, Amen.

CHAPTER 6

Grieving The Spirit

All throughout my life, my family constantly reminded me that my body is the temple of the Lord. Because the Holy Spirit lives in me, everything I do directly affects God because my body is His home. If I eat foods that are unhealthy or overindulge in alcohol or food, my body becomes the equivalent of a nasty dirty house. Now, I would never invite guests over if my house were untidy, so why would I invite God to live inside of me if my body is not clean? This teaching has helped me in my walk of abstinence for a few reasons: 1) I don't want fingerprints on my body, 2) I don't want other people's germs dirtying my temple, 3) I know that three's a crowd (me/him/Holy Spirit).

The saying that *the house we live in is not our own* is a cliché that has never been truer than when relating to our physical bodies. Yes, we live in these temples, but our bodies are on loan to us from God. We are HIS temples. Therefore, all that takes place in and to our bodies directly affects our Lord. And because the Holy Spirit lives within each of us who have accepted Christ as our Savior, the things we do affect the Holy Spirit within. When we drink alcohol excessively, we are physically harming our bodies. Likewise, when we ingest sin into our bodies, we are harming or grieving the Spirit. When we grieve the Spirit, His voice becomes distant and faint. The warning signals get softer and all of the red flags, those little reminders that keep us in check from doing wrong, become faint. I think my pastor best summed it up when he made an analogy between a woman's body and a priceless crystal vase. When people constantly handle the vase, fingerprints are left behind, which takes away from the beauty of the vase by covering its natural light. Likewise when men constantly handle our precious bodies, our light, the Holy Spirit, is covered in layers of filth, grime, and whatever else accompanies the sin. We are still the same beautiful creatures made by Him, but the cloak of sex and constant handling makes our beauty difficult to recognize.

Now to some of you, this may all sound like pulpit rhetoric, but believe me, this analogy and picture constantly remind me of how precious I am in the sight of God, and how important it is for me to stay focused on remaining *fingerprint-free*. Our bodies are holy places. Just imagine your body as the temple of the Holy Spirit, the place where God lives. Would you invite God into a dirty home? Once

He's there, would you invite over guests with whom you KNOW He doesn't want to keep company? That's exactly what happens when you have sex on the brain, constantly thinking about sex and how/why/when/with whom. Lascivious thought is the equivalent of having old newspapers and soggy cereal in sour milk in the middle of your living room. Having sex out of wedlock is the equivalent of inviting over guests that don't click with the Father. Now do you really want to do that? I don't think so, because if you're still reading this book, I believe that you WANT to walk in a lifestyle of abstinence. You want to maintain your virginity until God acknowledges a relationship between you and the mate He has for you.

I am reminded of the occurrence in the New Testament (Matt 21:12) where Jesus goes into the temple and, seeing the sin there, turns over tables and kicks people out. Jesus walked into His Father's house and *cleaned* house! In the holy place, there was gambling and cards, prostitution and a market, where people sold their goods. Because this was the place where God lived, the masses were out of order in letting such sinful practices take place. They were grieving the Spirit of God, which angered the Son of God. It was so important to Jesus that His Father's house be reverenced that He became enraged to the point of turning over tables. This is how we have to be with our bodies, ladies. *God lives here. Do you hear me? The Father LIVES inside each of us!* Yes, we are walking in earthly bodies, but this fact does not negate that we are spiritual beings having earthly experiences. Because the Holy Spirit takes up residence in us, we must work extra hard to ensure that He is comfortable in this home, which is our bodies. Inviting unwanted guests is Not AN OPTION. Haven't you ever heard that three's company? There's only room enough for you and the good Lord!

As I sit and try to think about examples of women who walked in virtue, without leaning and depending on the Proverbs 31 Virtuous Woman*[1], I am compelled to talk about Esther. The care that was taken in preparing her to become intimate with her king is one that I can equate to the preparation that we all go through at some point in our lives. Esther was set apart for quite some time (12 months) in preparation to come before the king. During that time, she was pampered with massages, scents, and overall grooming so that the king would be pleased when he saw her. And even with all this preparation, the truest preparation started long before her *appointed time,* with the maintenance of her virtue. Because she was a virgin, without the fingerprints of any other man, she was taken in as part of the king's court, which would later be scaled down to just Esther.

Usually the lessons on Esther all center around her walk of faith, which is indeed a strong testimony, but for the sake of our discussion, we will focus more on her preparations and success in not grieving the Holy Spirit. As is customary for Jewish women, Esther protected the Spirit within herself. She is described as being very beautiful, which means that she very possibly had to make the decision to say no to any offers that did not rest well with her Spirit. It is likely that she turned down a few dates and kisses and petting just to stay in line with what God had ordained for her life: marrying the King and saving the Jewish people from annihilation. She successfully kept the fingerprints off her vase. Not only did she succeed in not inviting unwanted guests into her Lord's house (her body), but she also spent time preparing herself and being prepared for the mate God had ordained for her life. To me her story reads as follows: *Walk in holiness. Don't bring anyone into your relationship with God without asking His permission (marriage). Spend the preparation period becoming a better you. Get your hair done. Look good. Smell good. (Esther 2:12-17)* In a nutshell, I think this interpretation of Esther's walk can serve as bold encouragement for those of us who are abstaining on a path that seems not to have welcomed many visitors before us. As long as we stay on this path and work hard not to grieve the Holy Spirit, we will be one step closer to having a full and *fulfilling* life.

Questions

1 **How do your daily actions affect the Holy Spirit living inside of you?**

2 **How can you protect the Holy Spirit in you like Esther protected the Holy Spirit in her?**

Challenge: For the next 2 weeks (14 days), I challenge you to practice living a life of preparation, not just for a man, but actually for yourself. Take time to pamper yourself everyday, if only for 15 minutes. Do something that YOU want to do for yourself. Paint your nails or change perfumes, but whatever it is, become more aware of yourself and life's little pleasures.

CHAPTER 7

Not a Dirty Word

Not that long ago, Pop singer Jennifer Lopez released a song with the "n" word in it. Because she isn't Black, the media and people all across the globe protested the song, it's lyrical content, and the singer herself. Suddenly the "n" word, *nigger,* stepped into the spotlight, as it does every now and then, sparking conversations and even incensing some to protest. People took a word that had been, until the time of the song's release, referenced in both a positive and negative connotation by many in the black community and brought to light the numerous negative definitions and detrimental cultural uses of the word. With all of the negative historical implications, the "n" word issue of late reminded everyone of the power of the tongue, the power of language, the power of the spoken word. And as I sat, watching the entertainment and music magazines chronicle the incident, my mind immediately turned to another word that causes knee-jerk responses, even when it shouldn't…VIRGIN.

The first time the word "virgin" really surfaced in my life, outside of my home, was in one of my Literature classes in high school when I studied Nathaniel Hawthorne's *The Scarlet Letter.* In this story, a woman (Hester Prynne) is required to wear an embroidered "A" (for adultery) whenever she is in public because she had conceived a child while she was yet married. In the class discussion of the book, I distinctly remember spending DAYS on the topic of virginity and it's affect on society during the setting of the book as well as at the time of that class. In the story setting, it's obvious that virginity was a "thing" looked upon in a positive light, unlike the way many viewed it during the time of my class. During the setting of the book, as well as during Biblical times, a woman's virtue was the most important part of her identity. A man's ultimate quest in life was securing a beautiful, virginal damsel to wed. In modern times, such is not the case. In the Bible, a woman who lost her virginity was stoned to death by the men in the community. These days, the word VIRGIN may as well be a four-letter word. Nobody wants to be called one because it's not cool. All of the music videos and songs support sexiness, sexy clothes, sexy dancing and just plain old sex. So how does one filter through all of the media distractions and learn to embrace the word and the lifestyle? I mean, this situation is so serious that it amazes me that there has been no hoopla over the "v" word as there was with the "n" word.

I believe that the beginnings of the dislike for the word and lifestyle began sometime during the feminist movement of the 70's. For so long, women in America had been taught to remain "pure" for their husbands, or so that someone would marry them. During the movement, one of the items on the agenda was creating a space for women to define themselves in and on our own terms. I believe that the definition started and ended with the vagina. Women "Reclaimed" their vaginas and in a sense reclaimed themselves. And while that action helped lay the foundation for much of the feminist work that was done, at some point the pendulum shifted far from the center and back-lashed against the choice of virginity and abstinence.

In my generation, virgin IS a dirty word. Nobody wants to be called one. Whatever you call me, just don't call me a virgin. Such connotations as "she's so not cool" or "she's so not cute" are attached to the word, so who in her right mind would want to be called one?

The last song that I can remember advocating abstinence is Janet Jackson's 80's hit single "Let's Wait A While", which, while it lasted for a year or so on the airwaves and helped me make it through a trying adolescent period, does NOT reach young people today…and there hasn't been anything else in mainstream since then. There are few entertainers and athletes of today, under 30 years of age, advocating abstinence, which probably has more to do with their not wanting to be attached to the stigma of the word than their actual sex practices. I know that there are some entertainers and athletes who are abstaining and who are virgins, but because it may take away from their images, they don't openly advocate the lifestyle to today's kids.

Since the apprehension towards the word is so widespread, here are a few of my suggestions for those dealing with the "v" word issue: 1) understand the value of having a good name, 2) come to grips with your choices for YOURSELF, 3) recognize that often times men prefer to marry virgins (so don't feel rushed), and 4) explore the positive associations of the word.

UNDERSTANDING THE VALUE OF HAVING A GOOD NAME

I remember when I was in middle school, junior high, and high school that there were some girls who were soooo popular, mainly because they put out. On more than one occasion, I was told by guys that I wasn't the kind of girl they'd take out, but rather the kind they'd take home to meet their mothers. Now of course when I was in that situation, I went home crying, not because I wasn't popular — because I was, but rather because I wasn't "that" type of girl. And I distinctly recall telling my mother and having her smile and say how great it was that guys thought that about me, which only made me more angry and upset. But in hindsight, I realize that having a "good" name was indeed a good thing, even though it meant meeting far more mothers than I ever cared to meet! Having a good name goes a long way. When I didn't even know that people were watching me, various adults in the community were, and by high school, I had maintained a track record for being a smart good girl, which garnered various scholarships and other forms of support as I prepared for college.

COME TO GRIPS WITH YOUR CHOICES FOR YOURSELF

Earlier I mentioned the feminist movement and the huge impact I believe it had on the perception of virginity. One of the ideals of that time, which still lingers today, centers around the use of the vagina. From all I've learned about the movement, women rallied around the notion of reclaiming one's vagina for oneself. To put it in a much simpler context, some people believed that a woman should maintain her virginity for the man in her life, or her future husband. The movement contradicted this notion by advocating that women begin to take ownership of their sexuality and free themselves from the ideology that previously existed regarding the need to "save oneself" for a man. In this small aspect, I agree with the movement. For years I was told by some of our society that I should save myself for my "husband" and honestly, this notion was and is not enough to convince me to abstain. Why should I deny myself immediate pleasure for some man who at this moment is nowhere near my life? After soul-searching one day, I resolved that I wouldn't save myself for my imaginary husband, but rather, I'd save myself *for* myself. I want to be able to walk into any room anywhere and be confident that there's no one there who knows me intimately or has seen the private me. I want to maintain my peace of mind, which is sometimes lost along with one's virginity. And when I DO have sex, I want to be able to rest in the comfort of knowing that I've made a right decision, not looking over my shoulder trying not to get caught or praying a pre-meditated prayer to God for forgiveness. So I think it's important to keep things in perspective along this journey and realize that abstinence is for the individual — it's for the soul. And it's not something that you can do for your "husband" or your pastor or your parents, but rather something that only you can do for *you*.

MEN ADORE VIRGINS

Even to the extent that you save yourself for yourself, keep in mind that many men love the mystery of a virgin.[2] I've seen it time and time again — men stare in amazement when I inform them that the party stops *here* because of my stance on sex. Few of them have actually laid eyes on a virgin in years (since their teens), and fewer of them have had a chance to converse with one. So if nothing else, the virgin status becomes a conversation piece and has led to more than one marriage proposal in my lifetime. I've found that as times change, men (to a certain degree) stay the same. The same ones who insisted upon marriage to a virginal damsel in Biblical times are still here in a different outfit, singing the same ol' song...There's a period that men go through where they really don't want to pursue a relationship with a virgin because they are more interested in having a relationship that includes sex, but as they mature and prepare to settle down, the idea of not having anyone's leftovers becomes more and more appealing. Now, when a guy reaches a point where he wants to settle down a little, he's attracted to the thing in you that's different — freshness and innocence. That "thing" is virginity…the same "thing" that was a dirty word only years before becomes a prized jewel now.

For so long I dreaded the sex conversations because I KNEW that my past history, or lack thereof, would come up and I just HATED saying the word. For me, it WAS a dirty word. Whenever the sex conversation came up, which was often during high school and college, I felt knots in my stomach because I was uncomfortable with how people would view me, and the same old questions that they always asked. Surprisingly, as I began to share the concept of this book with other people, and I actually began to feel more comfortable with the word "virgin", I also became more comfortable with myself. So when I write that I understand where you are, I do. When I state that I know what you're going through, it's true. I've been there, done that, and here's the souvenir. I believe that God left me in that state of virgin limbo and seemingly allowed all of my friends to move into another space just so that He could allow me to really feel where other young ladies are so that I would be better able to speak to your pains and honestly answer your questions…which I hope is happening for you now.

EXPLORE THE POSITIVE ASSOCIATIONS OF "VIRGIN"

For every negative vantage of the word "virgin", there exists a positive view. There are certain ideals that people think when they hear that a person is a virgin. People think that because you are not sexually active, you are associated with the following terms: Pure, clean, integrity, chaste, virtuous, meek (not to be confused with "weak"), strong willed, true to self, faithful, honest, trustworthy, and more! Just pick one and let it speak for you!

Questions

1 **How do you feel when you hear the word "virgin"? does it make you uncomfortable? Are you ashamed of the label? Or are you proud of the title?**

2 Take a second to be real with yourself. Why are you abstaining from sex? (God, family, self?)

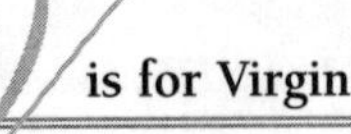

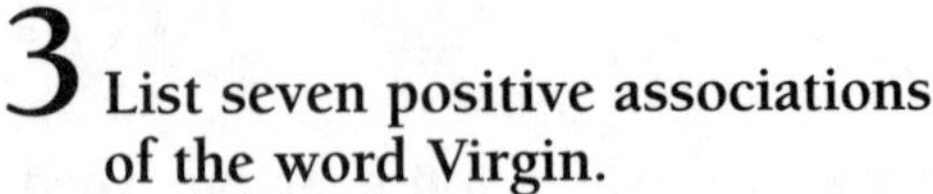

3 List seven positive associations of the word Virgin.

1) ____________________

2) ____________________

3) ____________________

4) ____________________

5) ____________________

6) ____________________

7) ____________________

Challenge: I challenge you to stop right this second and write down a list of all your reasons for not having sex, then put the list in your wallet (where you'd normally keep a condom) as a lifesaver in case of an emergency.

All of my reasons
for NOT having sex

CHAPTER 8

The Stress Test

By Jr. High School, many of my friends were already sexually active, so the "ALARM" has rang in my vicinity more than a few times. Surely you know which alarm I'm speaking of…the "I'm Late" alarm that goes off every few months from a friend whose period is late. I remember the first time this alarm went off. In Jr. High one of my friends called me into the restroom right at the beginning of recess to tell me, with tears running down her face, that her 'visitor' hadn't come that month. And at that time, I remember feeling like I was going to throw up, which had absolutely NOTHING on how she was feeling. Immediate thoughts of: *how am I going to tell my mom? My dad's gonna be so disappointed…right after he kills me. Can you believe he asked who else I'd been with like I sleep around or something? Will I have to quit school?* and many more…Can you imagine the thought of losing control of your life just for the sake of getting some? Just the thought alone puts knots in my stomach, so what if the shoe in this situation were on the other foot? Virginity and abstinence ensure that such stressful scenarios never happen to you.

By high school, the alarm was almost a common occurrence. At least once every month or so a friend or classmate, black or white, had to make the decision to either keep or abort her baby. The difference during those four years had more to do with the accessories of sex than the pregnancies. During this phase of life, STDs (sexually transmitted diseases) ran rampant. When the government reported statistics on HIV/AIDS for the state of Georgia, my region sat near the top of the list.

In the school district, we began to have more assemblies on sex and its effects on the mind and body, as well as the diseases that are carried from one person to the next. I think the best example ever given was the one that gave a break down how many people actually sleep with you when you have sex. If you have sex with one guy who has had sex with 3 people, you have actually been with four people. Because germs and bacteria are so small, some of them hide in the folds of the skin, regardless of how thoroughly a guy cleans himself. One of the main viruses, found in one of every three sexually active people, the human papilloma virus (HPV), can appear in several different forms because it has various strands which cause different symptoms, some of which include: genital warts, cervical legions, and even internal issues which may lead to cervical cancer. So just think, the one guy that you sleep with, who has slept with 3 other people (assuming they were all virgins), has opened you up to an incurable virus. And it's really easy to say or think that you won't get it if you have sex just one time because you're clean or cute or whatever excuse you chose, but the truth of the matter is that *anyone* can get it. Some of my friends, who are smart, cute, funny, clean, and sexually responsible, carry the virus…and so can you.

One of the biggest viruses that cause stress is HIV (human imuno deficiency syndrome). We all know about it and know ways to protect ourselves, but at the end of the day we also know that sometimes things happen. Here's the scenario: You're caught up in the moment and you don't have a condom or it breaks and you continue getting your grove on. Now what? Or you decide to have sex exclusively with your boyfriend who hasn't been tested, but because you are in a monogamous relationship, you think it's cool to do it unprotected, especially since you're on the pill. Now how do you think you'll feel when your doctor calls with news of your incurable disease? I'm not saying these things or giving you such vivid examples as a scare tactic because I realize that they don't work on most people. I'm simply trying to show you that life with sex is much more stressful than life without sex.

And the final stressful moment directly related to sex I think would be making the decision to keep or abort a pregnancy. If you ask most women about whether or not they'd have an abortion if they became pregnant out of wedlock, they'd probably say no and give all these reasons about life and the blessing of a child; however, if the situation arose whereby they found themselves pregnant, making only a certain amount of money, and not living up to the expectations they have for themselves, I think you might hear a different answer. The decision that has to be made is truly a grueling one. It's one where you're torn between yourself and yourself — a no-win situation in many cases. So if there were a way to keep from having that undue burden weighing on your shoulders, wouldn't you take it? I've always been one to learn from the mistakes of others. Why should I endure stress and struggles if I can see that a particular path didn't work for several people who tried it?

Another stress that young women put on themselves has everything to do with body image. Because sex starts for many people in an early adolescent stage of life, the way that we look, how we're shaped, our weight, becomes a big issue at an early age. I can't imagine growing up now and having to look like Britney Spears' or Beyonce's image. I went shopping earlier this month during the back-to-school sales, and almost every article of clothing was revealing. I couldn't believe it because I just think that the media hype can totally destroy a young person's image of self. So let me first say that you don't have to look like the women in the videos to be beautiful.

There's a song by India.Arie that does a wonderful job of dismantling the beauty myth that all women should look like Janet Jackson and J-Lo. In her song "Video", Arie croons: "I'm not the average girl from your video/ And I'm not built like a supermodel/ but I've learned to love myself unconditionally/ because I am a Queen," which should be a goal that each of us strives toward daily.

Secondly, adding sex to the equation of self-image issues, which most young women have at some point in their lives, only adds drama to the equation. If sex is supposed to be heightened by relaxation, how good can it be if you're all tense about what your body looks like and how it feels? So maybe waiting until a time when you're actually more mature and comfortable with yourself physically and emotionally will allow you the space needed to make the adult decisions that come along with the choice to have sex.

The final stress test of sex has to do with money and a generational poverty situation. For me, education was the way out; for some of you it may be sports or music. I busted my butt in school to make sure that I made the grades to qualify for scholarships. And when I even *think* of the effect a disease or a child might have had on my life, I get nervous. I never would have received all the awards that I received had I gotten pregnant from a premarital relationship. I know that some single mothers work really hard to succeed, and I think that's great if that's the situation you find yourself in, but just from watching my own single mother struggle, I would prefer to take the road less traveled. *I simply would not have been able to have the lifestyle that I have experienced if I had a child.* By age 25, I had received a bachelors and masters degree, vacationed in other countries, purchased a home, and worked on some really cool projects in my career. I truly believe that I escaped the curse of generational poverty because of the decisions I made regarding sex. Now I don't claim to have all the answers, but I firmly believe that the one answer I *can* share is abstinence.

Maybe this solution doesn't work for everyone, but it's at least worth a try. I can honestly say that it works for me and for most of the people I know who practice it. Of course I have my not-so-hot days, but on a whole, I think — matter of fact, I KNOW — I'm well worth the wait. I've given myself a chance to develop into a person that I like and of which I am proud. I haven't lost my identity in a mate and changed everything that I am to become what he wants me to become. I've been true to myself because I can be comfortable loving myself, knowing that there are no strings attached which, by my definition, dramatically reduces stress! And if you have made it through without having the scare of motherhood, an STD, the decision of an abortion, and the drama of dealing with your body image as it relates to your sexuality, then you've officially passed the stress test!

Questions

1 **What are some of the *sex factors* related to sex? How have you or your friends dealt with them?**

2 **How is sex affected by a poor self or body image?**

3 **What effect might sex out of wedlock have on your financial situation?**

CHAPTER 9

A Kept Woman

"Thou wilt keep him in perfect peace, whose mind is stayed on thee…" (Isaiah 26:3)

Just from looking at what's on television and in the music videos today, young women may be easily led into a life that includes having someone pay their bills for the glamorous life (a "kept" woman). In every Jay-Z video that I can remember seeing in recent years, there's always the guy who is paid out the butt and the beautiful women who live in his houses, party at his clubs, and sunbathe on his yacht. If these are the only images that a young woman is exposed to, then it's not strange that she would grow up expecting to be a kept woman. Who doesn't like nice cars and houses and fine jewelry, especially if it's free? But nothing in life is free, so let's take a moment to count the real costs.

In real life, we pay for everything we get. Nothing is just given to us. In most instances, if a guy buys you an outfit, he wants something in return, and that something is very likely to be sex. If he buys you a car, he expects the payment of sex. If he lets you live in his house, he wants 24/7 access to the bootie. Now while this lifestyle may be viewed by some as being o.k., I think of it more as prostitution. When a young woman is tempted by the fabulous lifestyle of the guy on TV, or the ghetto fabulous styles of the thug next door, it's very difficult for her to say no, when saying no will impair the short-term upgrade of her lifestyle. It's difficult for some women to say no to sex when the guy can drive them to the store for groceries when they don't have food in their own refrigerators or when they're riding the bus. I think most people can understand this plight that some women face in their very real lives, and I don't make light of these situations at all; however, there is another solution that I have found to help me during those times when I could have pimped myself and reaped immediate rewards, but decided against it.

The solution that I found during a time when I seriously considered being a *chickenhead* (a gold digging, athletic/entertainment groupie) is Jesus. Now of course this answer may sound trite and cliché-ish, but it's real. Almost every guy I dated in college had either inherited wealth or gained it through sports or the music industry. At any point in any of these relationships, I could have betrayed my body for the sake of making a come-up. I've heard some young women rationalize their choice of being a *chickenhead* in terms of *separation of mind and body.* They would convince themselves that sex was only about that one part of the body and had absolutely nothing to do with the rest of who they were. I've even heard explanations as deep as *"having sex to gain a better lifestyle equals an investment in the future."* For some young women, that's what it's all about. They have sex with a *baller,* get pregnant, and receive support until the end of time. And for some of them, this is enough, but for me, this lifestyle — this blatant self-prostitution — isn't enough…not that I didn't think about it in the lean times, but thank God there was another solution.

To be completely honest with you, the thought has definitely crossed my mind to just be a *trick,* which seems like it would be a heck of a lot easier than struggling everyday to pass classes and get into grad school, then find a job, etc. During those times, I would think that 15 minutes on my back in exchange for an upgraded lifestyle that didn't include struggling couldn't be all that bad. I mean, what did I really have to lose, besides my soul? And I think that's where the change came in. You know, all my life people had preached virginity to me, but their preaching was never the reason for my abstinence. There would always be a bigger reason, be it the fear of disease or the disdain for poverty, that actually kept me in check. But during the times when I seriously considered altering my lifestyle, the only solution came in the form of the most wonderful peace I've ever known.

I remember leaving a church service and returning to my project-looking apartment near the university where I did my graduate studies and thinking "God, there has to be more than this. I need to feel something from you that will keep me from doing some things that I KNOW aren't pleasing in your sight." And no sooner had I said this to the Lord than He hugged me. As I lay in bed, he gave me the biggest hug I've ever had. It was the type embrace that completely envelopes you and leaves you in perfect peace. This was the feeling that brought me through a particularly trying time on my path of virginity.

When I really sat down and talked with God about the reasons I was considering turning in my Vcard™, I broke down some things for Him. I told Him that I could be debt-free in a matter of moments, and He reminded me that He had already paid my debts on the cross. I told Him that I could move up from the project-looking apartments and into a plush big phat house, and He reminded me that He had a mansion with room enough for me. When I began to cry about the nice car that I could be driving, He reminded me of all the times He kept my old high school car from falling apart and promised that for every single thing I gave up for His sake, He'd give them back multiplied like He did for Job. When I cried in pain over the fact that all of my friends were getting married, He reminded me of Ruth who waited for God to work things out for her to marry Boaz — her kinsman who became her provider. And when I told Him that I didn't want to be 40 years old having my first child and that my clock was ticking (at the ripe age of 24), He spoke to me like He did to Sarah, Abraham's wife, who was barren for almost a century! And when I finally lay before Him, all cried out, He wiped away my tears and sent me on a mission to gain more experiences that could be put in this book.

My conversation with God started a very long time ago, and to date, He has been a keeper of His word. He keeps me daily, and I don't have to compromise my lifestyle or my body to reap the benefits of His blessings. The things that I thought my "man" would do for me in exchange for sex are done by the only Man in my life right now — Jesus. My bills are always paid — on time. I'm happy living in a comfortable and safe environment. And at night, when I go to sleep, I know that the price for all that I have has been paid in full.

I would really like to encourage each of you to take a moment and assess the things that are going on in your life. Find out where you are, and then map out where you'd like to be. I dare you to actually *try* God and see that He won't fail you. It may seem easier to give up that most intimate part of yourself for the sake of making a come-up, but it's really a lot harder than you may think because what you're selling is more than just a bag of treats — it's your soul.

Questions

1 **If you could have any lifestyle and the cost was already paid (by God), what would be included? paint your dream world and now give God your heart's desires.**

2 **Explain "separation of mind and body" in your own terms.**

3 **Make a list of God's promises to you and check them off each time He keeps one, until your list is complete.**

"Delight yourself also in the Lord;
and He will give you the desires of your heart" Ps 37:4

Epilogue — Consequences

A few years ago at my church's annual Youth Conference, The Movement, youth teachers Lisa Bolden and Robin May shared a wonderful course study on the consequences of pre-marital sex and "almost-sex". As a topic, they chose "Almost *Does* Count", and shared true stories to equip teens with adequate information to help them make sound decisions. The following pages are taken from their session.

DEALING WITH THE FALLOUT

How far do *you* think is too far? Do you think it's ok to kiss, as long as there's no tongue involved? Do you think it's ok to let someone touch your vagina, as long as there's no penetration by a penis? Do you think there are some things that you can do that are without consequence and some things that you just can't do? Let me tell you a true story about a young male virgin who decided to save himself for marriage. For the sake of this conversation, we'll change his name to Craig and his wife's name to Tisa.

When Craig was in high school, he was quite the nerd — you know, not all that cute, not the most popular guy on campus. At that time in his life, he made the decision to maintain his virginity, which wasn't all that challenging since he hadn't grown into his looks yet. He had a heart after God and wanted to only have one sexual partner, that being his wife whenever he finally married. He had made his decision and was adamant about sticking to it. But then…you know there has to be a "but"…He grew a little bit, his height finally catching up to his shoe size, and actually turned out to be quite handsome. And that's where his problems began.

With his newfound attractiveness and popularity, Craig began to be noticed by the cute girls at school. He'd take them out on dates, but because he had made a decision to keep his virginity in tact, he set limits to what he would and would not do. Initially, he would just kiss the girls on the cheek and maybe hold their hand. This progressed into kissing on the mouth, which inevitably led to French kissing with the tongue. From there he moved on to rubbing the back, arms, and legs, which of course led to petting and subsequently heavy petting. Then Craig began to feel convicted, or guilty, because although he wasn't actually having sex, he was going almost all the way with a lot of women he didn't plan to marry…until he met the woman he knew would be his wife for ever…to grow old and die with.

When Craig met Tisa, he just knew. He knew that she was the one he'd been saving himself for. They dated for two years before they were married, and they continued to do the same things that Craig had been doing with all those other women. They believed that as long as they weren't actually having sex, it was ok to pleasure themselves, especially since they were planning to get married eventually anyway. After the two-year dating/engagement period, they were married and excited about their honeymoon. They were both virgins, technically, until they consummated their marriage.

Yes, they were both virgins, but do you think that their behavior was pleasing to God? Do you think it ever dawned on them that maybe they were grieving the Holy Spirit by their actions…inviting guests over when He didn't want guests over? Do you think the angels that watch over us, the heavenly host, just closed their eyes or turned their backs during all of the foreplay that took place before the marriage? Yes, they were virgins, but do you think God was pleased with Craig and Tisa's sexual life? Did they do anything wrong, or do you think their actions were ok?

Craig and Tisa's actions bring to mind the title of R&B singer Brandy's hit song, *Almost Doesn't Count.* While the context of her song deals with relationships and not sex, the title captures one of the primary notions that many people have regarding sex: **if you don't do it all the way, then it doesn't count.** If it's just kissing, then it doesn't count. If I make all of the plans to seduce my man, but something comes up to prevent it from happening, then it doesn't count. If we try to have sex, but for whatever reason he can't make it fit, then it doesn't count. We have so many scenarios that we create to fulfill the lust and physical needs that we have, stopping just short of sex. And we say that because it's not sex, it doesn't count.

Surely that's what Craig and Tisa thought when they made out before they were married. And since "almost sex" doesn't count against us, there should be no consequences, right?...Wrong.

Newton's Law of Motion states that *for every action, there's an equal and opposite reaction.* Many times, when we do things, we know that there will be some type of reaction that follows. If you pimp slap somebody, it's very VERY likely that the person is going to retaliate. That person may cuss you out. She may punch you. She might even call the police to put a restraining order on you AFTER she beats you down. And however unlikely this may sound, she might let you slide until a later date — when you forget about it...then she just might sneak you. In all of those scenarios, you would expect a response of some sort because you initiated the *chain of events* by pimp slapping her. And you will also know that you can't choose what that person's reaction will be, so you can't *choose* your consequence. The same rule applies with God. When we do things that are not in His will — also known as SIN, there will be a consequence.

On Craig and Tisa's wedding night, they consummated the marriage, but not without facing some challenges. What should have been the most beautiful night — becoming one on the marriage bed, which is undefiled — was anything but. On that night, Craig couldn't enter Tisa's body, and when he finally did, the sex only lasted for about TWO minutes. Can you imagine the disappointment? You've waited all these years for something like *this* to happen?

The couple initially thought that the problems were occurring because of nerves, but still three months into the marriage, these same problems persisted. Then they got worse.

After seeking medical attention and counseling, the couple learned that Tisa suffered from *vaginismus* and *inorgasmia,* which causes the vagina to close in a vice-like grip and prohibits arousal, respectively. Meanwhile, Craig suffered from *impotence,* which caused him to ejaculate prematurely. At counseling, they learned that the impotence was caused by masturbation, his release after a heavy petting session. His body had been conditioned to reach a peak with no release, so when there *was* finally an opportunity for release, the result became two-minute sex sessions with his wife. Like her husband, Tisa had also conditioned her body to react to the petting, and not actual sex. With the heavy petting, she trained her vaginal muscles to relax and contract to a certain point, but then to close up. The starting and stopping of heavy petting conditioned her body to stop at the point of penetration, the result being that she could not receive her husband when it was time to do so. Her pre-sex activity also trained her body to become moist, but then to dry up at a certain time in the petting process…the starting/stopping thing. So although Craig and Tisa thought that what they were doing was ok since it wasn't sex, they still had a consequence to face. *Almost DOES Count.*

We sometimes think that if we do a "small" sin, like petting, then we will have a small consequence. And likewise, if we commit a "big" sin, like sex, we will have a slightly bigger consequence. And more than anything else, we hope that if we ask for forgiveness, we won't have any consequence at all. But if you take a moment to read Galatians 5:16-21, you'll notice that several sins are listed, yet the punishment is the same for them all. God doesn't see sin as BIG or little.

> *"This I say then, Walk in the Spirit, and ye shall not fulfill the lust of the flesh. For the flesh lusteth against the Spirit, and the Spirit against the flesh: and these are contrary the one to the other: so that ye cannot do the things that ye would. But if ye be led of the Spirit, ye are not under the law. Now the works of the flesh are manifest, which are these;* ***Adultery, fornication, uncleanness, lasciviousness, Idolatry, witchcraft, hatred, variance, emulations, wrath, strife, seditions, heresies, Envyings, murders, drunkenness, revellings, and such like:*** *of the which I tell you before, as I have also told you in time past, that* ***they which do such things shall not inherit the kingdom of God****" (Galatians 5: 16-21)*

To God, sin is sin, and HE decides the consequence. Just like you wouldn't be able to decide the consequence from the girl you pimp slap, you can't choose the consequence of your sin. God does that all on His own.

But there *is* something that you *can* choose. You alone have the options of life and death as choices that you can make. In Deuteronomy 30 God tells us that He has placed before us life and good, and death and evil. If our hearts are turned toward Him, then we will receive His blessing. If our hearts are turned away from Him, we will receive His curse. Those are the only two options we have from which to choose.

For Craig and Tisa, they thought that they were choosing *life and good* because of their decision to maintain their virginity. They never imagined that the consequences for their actions would actually affect their marriage bed, which they held in such high regard. For them, they forsook the commands of God and actually chose *death and evil.* Their consequences were serious. Consequences usually are.

With Robin and her husband Lee, the consequences were not quite as dramatic. They were together for nine years before they married — nine years that allowed for everything, except the act of sex. So while this marriage started off nothing like Craig and Tisa's, in terms of the consequences, Robin and Lee soon found themselves sitting in the middle of boredom after only two months of marriage. Because they had experimented with foreplay for years, their consequence came in the form of boredom. The great news for them was that there's was an easy fix — just thinking up more creative foreplay. Yet even in all that, there was still the issue of Lee's sexual past. Robin was a virgin when they married, but Lee wasn't. For her, she questioned whether or not he was comparing her to some of the other women whenever they had sex. And while both couples have healthy sex lives now, their generous transparency teaches us that we really *can't* choose our consequences. For some, the consequence may be acquiring an STD (yes, you can catch something without going all the way). For others it may be AIDS.

And yet still for those like Craig and Tisa, the consequence may be *impotence, vaginismus, and inorgasmia.* You can choose your action, but you can't choose God's reaction.

One of the struggles that we face in our society, one that makes it even harder for us to make the right decisions is that we are taught that it's ok to please ourselves. From commercials and television shows to music and videos, the resounding message is that we should seek to please ourselves in all things. From the Sprite commercial featuring Kobe Bryant, which asks us *who we're going to listen to,* then tells us to *listen to ourselves and obey our thirst,* to Juvenile's "Slow Motion" and Petey Pablo's "Freek-a-leek", not to mention BET's and MTV's after-hours programming, there seems to be no end to society inviting us to indulge in our flesh. Then there's multi-platinum Rap artist Nelly, who tells us that it's ok to take off our clothes if we're hot. Now please note that I love the Nelly song. The track is hot and the chorus is catchy, but when I look at the lyrics, I know that it's not a logical decision to take off all your clothes just because you're hot. If you're in a club and you get hot, do you really take off all your clothes? And what would be the consequences if we actually *did* take off all our clothes just because we were hot? Would you end up in jail for indecent exposure? Would you be groped by the guy dancing beside you? Is it really ok to just do whatever pops into your mind that you'd like to do?

Romans 12:1-2 says: *I beseech ye therefore, brethren, by the mercies of God, that ye present your bodies a living sacrifice, holy, acceptable unto God, which is your reasonable service.*

And be not conformed to this world: but be ye transformed by the renewing of your mind, that ye may prove what is that good, and acceptable, and perfect will of God. With this scripture, God is admonishing us to be an original, not a carbon-copy of what society says is popular in terms of behavior and customs. Let God transform you into a new person by changing the way you *think,* so that you can know God's good and perfect will for your life. Once you figure out what God's intention is for you, you can then go out and show others by example that listening to the Spirit is far more important than listening to the flesh. We can let society know that *almost DOES count!!!*

Now for some of you, there's still a pressing question on your mind. You're thinking, "That's all fine and well for Craig and Tisa, but I still don't know *how far is too far*". So here's a sidebar: Ask yourself if you would participate in whatever you're doing in front of your daddy, mother, pastor and the good Lord. If you wouldn't do it in front of them, that's your sign to draw the line. And if you're asking that question, you should take a moment to explore and change your mindset. In order to restore your paradigm, or way of thinking, to what God originally intended, there are four things that you should consider: 1) the desire to have sex is normal, but you must find contentment in your singleness, 2) there is a deposit of wealth in you that was put there by God, 3) there is a purpose/vision for your life, and 4) you need friends who will hold you accountable.

REALIZE THAT THE DESIRE FOR SEX IS NORMAL, BUT YOU MUST FIND CONTENTMENT IN YOUR SINGLENESS

In Phillipians 4:11, Paul writes a letter to the church of Phillipi admonishing them in the things of God. What I find most striking is his comment on contentment. In verse 11 he writes, *"Not that I speak in respect of want: for I have learned, in whatsoever state I am, therewith to be content"*. Paul says that he *learned* to be content, which means that there was a process through which he was worked towards being content in whatever state he found himself. That says so much to me because it shows that being single and content is not an unachievable goal. However it is something that I will have to work towards. In the season on singleness, there will be some bumps in the road — like those experienced by Craig and Tisa, but we can *learn* to be content even in this period of our lives.

REALIZE THAT THERE IS A DEPOSIT OF WEALTH IN YOU

Earlier in the book, we talked about our bodies being treasures of God, having hidden treasures in our earthen vessels (II Cor. 4:7). The treasure that shines from the inside is there as a testimony of God's glorious power, and not our own. We should live a lifestyle that shows people *why* we were created, which is to give God the glory. If you *know* that you're valuable, you'll carry your gift (which is your body) like you *know.* If someone gave you an envelope with a MILLION dollars, but told you not to spend it until a certain time, you'd be different. You'd act differently. You'd walk differently. You'd talk differently. And you'd certainly be more careful about choosing your friends. People around you would probably think you're crazy, but *you* would know that your status had changed. And everyone would see your attitude change. You have a treasure inside of you that's worth so much more than a million dollars, so *act* like you *know!*

REALIZE THAT THERE IS A PURPOSE AND VISION FOR YOUR LIFE

Once you recognize that there is a treasure inside of you, you need to know what it is for. Proverbs 29:18 states that *"Where there is no vision, the people perish..."*. You have to *know* that if God thought enough of you to give you such a tremendous treasure, He has a purpose in mind for you — one that He had for you even before the very foundations of the world. It's up to you to listen closely to His voice to find out what His vision is for you. Even if you were given that envelope with a million dollars, you'd need to have a plan for its use, which means that you'd have to know the purpose for that money. Ideally that plan would include investments, trust funds for your future children, gifts to your church, family and friends, support for your community and more. The same is expected for the treasure housed inside of you. Your *treasure* should be re-invested in those around you who you mentor, with some of your talents and gifting set aside for your future children, the church, your family and friends, and the community. And all of these places can be touched and made better by your gift, but you must first recognize your treasure and figure out the specifics of God's plan for you. Giving away your *treasure* is the equivalent of throwing away your million-dollar envelope!

REALIZE THAT YOU NEED FRIENDS TO HOLD YOU ACCOUNTABLE

In an earlier chapter, we discussed the need for friends who will pray for you and help keep you on track. When I sat with Robin and Lisa, I saw yet another way that friends should hold each other accountable. Robin and Lisa were roommates for a couple of years, during the time that Robin was engaged to be married. Although Robin is older than Lisa, Lisa took her responsibility seriously in terms of holding Robin accountable for her actions. If Robin and her fiancé, now husband, were in the room with the door closed after the streetlights were on, Lisa would knock on the door and have them open it. Now of course to me this sounds like a great inconvenience, but in actuality, Lisa's level of commitment to her friendship with Robin serves as a living testament of the covenant relationships we're *supposed* to have with each other.

There are several occurrences in the Bible where friendship is the centerpiece, but one excellent example is found in Mark 2:1-5. In this instance, a man born with palsy was brought to Jesus by four of his friends. They couldn't reach Jesus because of the crowd, so they uncovered the roof and lifted their friend over the wall and down through the now-removed ceiling. Verse 5 states that "*When Jesus saw their faith, he said unto the sick of the palsy, Son, thy sins be forgiven thee*". It wasn't by the man's faith that Jesus healed him, but rather by the faith of his friends who believed enough to get him to Jesus for healing. Those are the type friends we need to have. Likewise, those are the type friends we should strive to be. Sometimes in this walk of abstinence, our legs may become a little shaky. It is at these times that we need friends surrounding us who have enough faith to lay our case before the Lord.

Another scripture that references the need for friends is found in Ecclesiastes 4:9-12. It states:

> *"Two are better than one; because they have a good reward for their labour. For if they fall, the one will lift up his fellow: but woe to him that is alone when he falleth; for he hath not another to help him up. Again, if two lie together, then they have heat: but how can one be warm alone? And if one prevail against him, two shall withstand him; and a threefold cord is not quickly broken."*

So if the Bible tells us that two are better than one, maybe we should really take that into consideration, just like Lisa and Robin.

Now let's take a look at some practical applications of these principles.

HOW DO YOU BEGIN TO UNDERSTAND YOUR TREASURE?

The first step in understanding the fullness of your *treasure* is to get acquainted with the Word of God, which will teach you what He says about your treasure. Meditate on this Word Day and Night. You may want to begin by reading 2 Peter 1, 2 Corinthians7, and Ephesians 1.

The second step is to reaffirm God's promises for your life each day. You can stand in the mirror and speak the scriptures that you've read into your life. Gospel singing duo MaryMary has a song on their CD, *Incredible,* entitled "Little Girl". One of the lines in the song tells the little girl to look in the mirror and say that she loves herself. I think this one statement is profound because it is affirming for the little girl in all of us *what* God thinks of us when He looks at us…that He loves us and we're beautiful and precious in His sight.

The third step is to pray and ask God to give us His mindset about who we are — changing our own. You don't know what to pray? Check out Romans 8:26. This scripture states: *"Likewise the Spirit also helpeth our infirmities: for we know not what we should pray for as we ought: but the Spirit itself maketh intercession for us with groanings which cannot be uttered."* So even during those times when you don't know what to say or what to pray, God's got your back through His Holy Spirit.

HOW DO YOU GET A VISION FOR YOUR LIFE?

When first beginning your search for God's vision for your life, you should take a time out. This theory may sound kind of crazy at first glance, but really, that's what you should do. Spend some time with yourself, making a list of all the things you would do without being paid to do them.

What is it that you LOVE to do? What could you see yourself doing for the rest of your life? If money were no object (and it's not, since our Father is rich beyond measure), what would you be doing right now? Whatever your answer, that's your passion...the thing that brightens your day by just thinking about it. I love to sing. I remember being a little girl and just singing allllll the time. I'd use anything as my microphone and I'd make up songs and entertain my family with them. I'd also make up stories and tell them. These are the things that I'd do for free. What about you?

The second way to recognize your passion is by serving in the church. Because we're young and single, we have more time to dedicate to the work of the church than do those who have familial responsibilities. While you're working in the church, you can spend that time learning more about what you love to do!

A final means by which to discover your destiny is to simply ask God to reveal it to you. Pray and ask Him what it is that He ordained for you to do before you were even born. Just make sure that when you ask Him the question, you stick around long enough to hear His answer...it seems that when we pray to God, we usually do all of the talking. So be sure to slow down long enough to hear His answer.

HOW DO YOU MAINTAIN OR GAIN ACCOUNTABLE RELATIONSHIPS?

We've talked about the importance of friendship and accountability, so now there's nothing left but to do it. When you set out on the path to find accountability, you should first ask God who it is that's He's connected you to. We tend to have many friends, but not all of them are the people He has chosen to walk by our sides through life. You need someone with whom you're walking side-by-side, someone who's a little bit ahead of you, and someone who's a couple of steps behind you. The one who's by your side will help keep you on track on those crazy days when your heart wants to do right, but your body is in rebellion. The friend who walks in front of you will be there to serve as a guide because she has been where you are going. She will be able to impart wisdom and life into you to help you avoid life's boobie-traps. And then there will be the friend who walks behind you, the one you mentor to help guide her through, or steer her away from, the path you've already taken. These are the necessary friends. Just ask God to show you who they are in your life.

Once He points them out to you, it is your responsibility to verbalize to them that you *need* them to play an active role in your life. You have to express to them the need for transparency. You need to be able to be completely honest with them about your struggles, and be receptive to the feedback they give you.

In your male-female relationships, there are a couple of points you should take into consideration regarding accountability. First, you should re-consider going on one-on-one dates that are not in PUBLIC places. Or better yet, give the double-date a try. It's so easy to slip up when it's just you and that little cutie in the car on *Lover's Lane*. Public and group dates can help you stay out of trouble. Secondly, don't be a fool and forget your nature. If you know a kiss is dangerous for you, then steer clear!

WHAT DO I DO IF I'VE ALREADY GONE "THERE"?

The BIG question...OK, so you've gone "there", meaning sex. You've had sex, now what? How do you get back on track with God? First you have to repent, which means that you ask God for forgiveness and then STOP doing what you were doing. When God forgives us, He cleanses us from that sin through the blood He shed on the cross. Now the big thing with repentance is the part where you TURN away from what you're doing. That's so important because many times, we stand before God and ask Him to forgive us, and He does. Then we turn right back around a couple of days later, do the same thing AGAIN, and ask for forgiveness AGAIN. That's called having a reprobate mind, one that refuses to do that which is moral. Romans 1:28 states that for those who would rather continue in sin than follow the commands of Christ, God *"gave them over to a reprobate mind"*. This means that because they wanted to continue to practice sin, He would let them. That's why it's so important that you take Him seriously. If you're sorry for the sins you've committed through sexual immorality, ask for forgiveness, then change your ways.

The second step is to make a commitment to a friend, parent, or youth leader that you will change your behavior. These people will hold you accountable for your actions and words. And finally, in all that, make sure that you stay repentant. Continually seek God's face for your weak spot, so that He will continue to strengthen you in this area.

I have several friends who have given their hearts and bodies back to God, which is such a commendable thing. I sometimes use ice cream as an analogy for sex. I love ice cream. It tastes great, although it's not good for me. I can't imagine not being able to eat ice cream. Even more than that, I don't know how well I would fare if I had to put a self-imposed restraint on my indulging in ice cream. When I think about my friends who have stopped having sex, I think that they have to feel about sex kinda how I feel about ice cream. The fact that some of them just stopped cold-turkey truly amazes me. Because they are successful in their pursuit of abstinence, I can stand in agreement with you that you, too, can be successful in your vow of purity.

Conclusion Prayer

In this last page of what I hope has been both a learning and supportive tool for your growth and journey down the path of virginity, I would like to leave a prayer with you to help you in your decision-making process and to strengthen your walk. Please refer to this page daily until you reach a point where you feel strong enough to walk this path alone…and even then, it won't kill you to refer back to it as a vitamin for your soul.

Dear Lord,

I come thanking you for all your blessings that you've bestowed upon me. First, thank you for the precious gift of life that you've so freely given to me. Had you not died on the cross for me, I would not be able to walk this path of abstinence in victory. So thank you.

Right now I ask that you continue to strengthen my spirit and my mind so that I can continue to preserve my body for your glory. I pray that you keep me in your will as you increase my will to abstain from sex until I'm married.

Lord at this time, I ask that you help my flesh put up a barrier against outside sources, such as TV and music, that may sway me in a direction other "than the one I have chosen. Please help me to filter out any words or images that may seep into my spirit and change my mind about my decision.

God, I rely completely on you. I know that you are a keeper, so I release my flesh into your able hands. Please help my spirit control my flesh. And Lord, please help my mind stay on you, as I walk in the path that I've chosen for my life. If at any point I go astray, please guide me back into the warmth of your embrace.

All these blessings I pray in your son Jesus' name, Amen.

End Notes

1 In Proverbs chapter 31, King Lemuel's mother gives him advice on the type of woman he should choose as a wife. She describes this woman as a virtuous one; one who keeps her home life and work life in perfect balance, all the while making her husband feel like a king. The "virtuous woman" creates a safe place for her husband's heart, finds fabrics and works with her hands, brings her food from far away, wakes up while it's still dark to feed her household, buys property and plants a vineyard, stays up late working, helps the poor, sews clothing for her family, makes clothes for others and sells them, speaks with wisdom and kindness, and is not idle. And her reward for all this work is praise from her children and husband. Whew, I'm tired just typing all of these things. That's what I call bringing home the bacon and frying it up in a pan. Sometimes this list of things that make a woman "virtuous" seems unrealistic and difficult to achieve. I prefer to look at this chapter as a goal sheet, instead of mandatory sentence of womanhood.

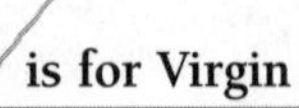

is for Virgin

2 “There be three things which are too wonderful for me…the way of an eagle in the air; the way of a serpent upon a rock; the way of a ship in the midst of the sea; **and the way of a man with a virgin**” (Prov 30: 18-19).

Vocabulary NaVigator —
(ALSO KNOWN AS THE GLOSSARY)

Alarm — the moment of panic when someone realizes she may be pregnant (usually around the time of a missing period)

Baller — a man who is iced-out in jewelry, has flashy cars, money and a big PHAT house. This type man is known for treating women like objects, to be acquired and used. They generally offer women a glamorous lifestyle in exchange for sex and power. Also referred to as "balla".

Booga — an ugly man! Ok, "ugly" is kinda harsh, so we'll just call him "aesthetically challenged".

Breaking Points — the state of mind and BODY where one more touch or look, etc. will lead straight to sex.

Cadillac Escalade — THE dream car (actually, it's an s.u.v., but it's absolutely fabulous!)

Communication G.A.P. — Gaming And Playing (also referred to as the "GAP") is the act of pretending not to know what "he" is saying to you so that you can manipulate the situation and get more from "him" than "he's" prepared to give.

Cut up, the — sex

Emotionally Unavailable — when a person is physically present, but seems to be in another place mentally and emotionally because of prior life experiences (and a million other things that allow them to detach themselves from loved ones).

Fat Factor — a syndrome which allows women to *hide* themselves from the attention of males by choosing to be overweight or dress in clothes that suggest a larger body shape.

Fits — specific times of the month during the menstrual cycle, when the mind loses the battle for control of the body's sexual urgings.

Grown up, the — sex

Hit it — sex

Put Out — sex

Red Flags — warning signals from the small voice inside

Test Drive — *widely accepted definition:* sampling your partner sexually to make sure you're compatible prior to marriage; *my definition:* learning specific long-term details about the person with whom you're in a relationship

Trick — a person who trades sex for Baller BENEFITS (these benefits may include, but are not limited to: expensive dinner, international vacations, access to a house, access to a car, shopping sprees, jewelry, etc.)

Visitor — Period

X — the drug ecstasy (a synthetic drug popular in younger circles; often the drug of choice at Raves); makes user feel "happy" and "loving"; destroys brain cells.

The Rules

1 *Don't put yourself in compromising positions.*

2 *Flee temptation (but if you have issues, just call Jesus!!!).*

3 *Pray to be kept by God.*

4 *Know your limitations.*

5 *Know your ovulation cycle and STAY HOME during the "warning' period.*

6 *Reinforce your choices with scripture.*

7 *Surround yourself with friends who encourage you in your decision.*

About the Author

Chiquita Lockley is a daughter, niece, granddaughter, sister and friend who enjoys helping others as a non-profit consultant. She has spent time working with and mentoring young people from various walks of life. She received a Bachelor of Arts degree in English from Spelman College and a Master of Arts degree in Film Studies from Emory University. In her free time, she enjoys singing and writing songs. Chiquita is a member of New Birth Missionary Baptist Church, in Lithonia, GA, and Delta Sigma Theta Sorority, Inc. She resides in Decatur, GA, just outside of Atlanta.

Other Recommended Books

by BISHOP EDDIE L. LONG

The Elect Lady (2005 release)
What A Man Wants, What A Woman Needs
I Don't Want Delilah, I Need You
The Power Of A Wise Woman

by P. BUNNY WILSON

Knight In Shining Armour
Liberated Through Submission

by BISHOP T.D. JAKES

Daddy Loves His Girls

by DR. JUANITA BYNUM-WEEKS

Matters of the Heart

Notes

Notes

Notes